NUMBER SIGNS for EVERYONE

NUMBERING
in
American Sign Language

DawnSignPress

With 90-minute DVD by Cinnie MacDougall

DawnSignPress
San Diego, CA

NUMBER SIGNS FOR EVERYONE: Numbering in American Sign Language
Copyright © 2008 DawnSignPress
All Rights Reserved.

No part of this book (except brief quotations to be included in a review) may be reproduced, stored in a retrieval system, or transmitted by any means, electronic, mechanical, photocopying, recording, or otherwise, without written permission from the publisher.

Manufactured in the United States of America
Published by DawnSignPress

SIGN MODELS

Sandra Ammons   Ben Bahan   Tina Jo Breindel   John Reid

Joe Dannis   In Hwa Reisig   Bob Hiltermann   Cinnie MacDougall   Ken Mikos

10 9 8 7 6 5 4 3 2 1

ATTENTION

Quantity discounts available.
For information, please contact:

DawnSignPress

6130 Nancy Ridge Drive
San Diego, CA 92121
858-625-0600 V/VP 858-625-2336 FAX
ORDER TOLL FREE 1-800-549-5350
www.dawnsign.com

Table of Contents

Introduction — *vii*

Chapter 1: How Many
- **1.1** Numbers 0–10 — *1*
- **1.2** Numbers 11–30 — *2*
- **1.3** Numbers 31–109, and Multiples of 100 — *3*
- **1.4** Emphasis — *9*
- **1.5** Large Numbers and Mixed Numbers — *9*
- **1.6** Approximations — *11*
- **1.7** Number Representation — *12*
- **1.8** Quantifiers — *13*

Chapter 2: Money
- **2.1** Cents — *17*
- **2.2** Fingerspelling Cents — *18*
- **2.3** Dollars — *19*
- **2.4** Mixed Money Signs — *20*
- **2.5** Approximate Money Signs — *21*

Chapter 3: Finances
- **3.1** Payment and Spending — *23*
- **3.2** Income — *25*
- **3.3** Losses — *26*
- **3.4** Finance-Related Signs — *27*
- **3.5** Finance-Related Occupations — *29*

Chapter 4: Measurements
- **4.1** Numerical Signs Showing Quantity and Frequency — *31*
- **4.2** Quantifiers — *32*
- **4.3** Fractions — *33*
- **4.4** Body Measurements — *35*
- **4.5** Vehicle-Related and Computer-Related Signs — *40*

Chapter 5: How Long
- **5.1** Seconds — *43*
- **5.2** Minutes, Hours, Days, Weeks, and Months — *43*
- **5.3** Years — *46*
- **5.4** Duration — *47*

Chapter 6: How Often
- **6.1** Numerical Time Frequency Signs — *51*
- **6.2** Other Frequency Signs — *54*

Chapter 7: When
- **7.1** Signs for Telling Time — *57*
- **7.2** Time Estimates — *58*
- **7.3** The Timeline in ASL — *61*
- **7.4** Year and Date Signs — *67*

Chapter 8: Age
- **8.1** Age — *69*

Chapter 9: Sports
- **9.1** Sports-Related Vocabulary — *75*
- **9.2** Placement and Scores — *78*

Chapter 10: Where, Which
- **10.1** Location — *81*
- **10.2** Places — *83*
- **10.3** Rank or Order in Family — *83*
- **10.4** Ordinal Numbers — *85*

Chapter 11: Personal Numbers
- **11.1** Identification Numbers — *87*
- **11.2** Signs for Specific Things — *89*

Chapter 12: Scientific Numbers
- **12.1** Scientific Numbers — *91*

INTRODUCTION

HOW TO USE THIS BOOK

NUMBER SIGNS FOR EVERYONE gives basic information about how numbers are used in American Sign Language (ASL). In twelve chapters you will be introduced to basic number signs such as counting from 1 to 10, and complex number signs, such as how to describe the placement of a team in a volleyball tournament.

Over one thousand illustrations of number signs constitute the majority of the book. Illustrations can never take the place of learning signs from a live instructor or from interacting with signers, but the sign illustrations do have detailed content that will help you learn to form the sign correctly.

HOW TO READ THE ILLUSTRATIONS

The basic four parameters of every sign are *handshape*, *palm orientation*, *location*, and *movement*. When evaluating a sign illustration, first identify how each of these elements contributes to the sign.

HANDSHAPE

There are approximately forty commonly used handshapes in ASL and many others that are seen only occasionally. Many of the handshapes appear similar, but are in fact very specific.

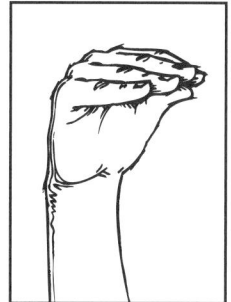 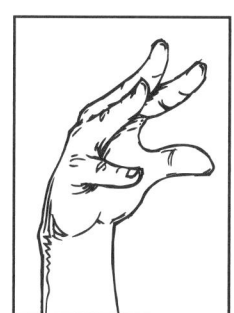 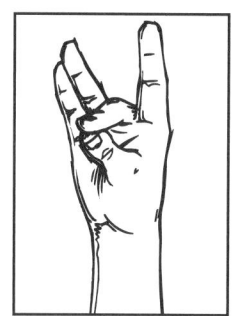 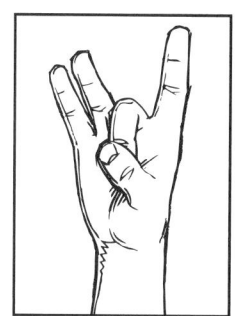

INTRODUCTION

The following chart shows the common handshapes for ASL.

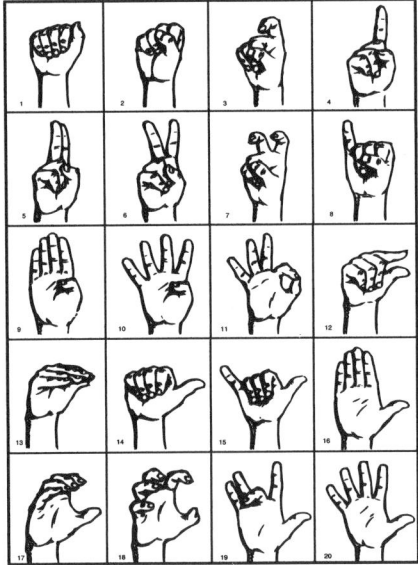
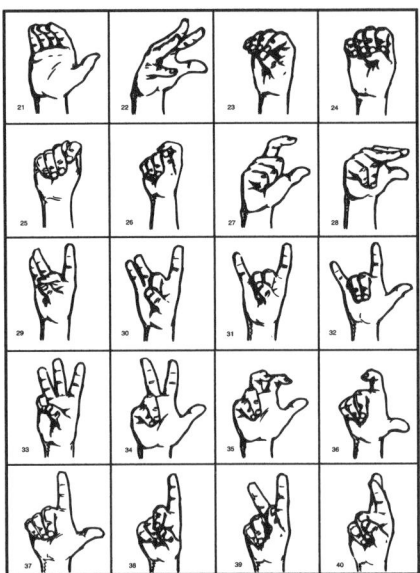

PALM ORIENTATION

Orientation of the hands, such as palm facing outward, palm facing inward, and thumb side of the hand pointing up or down, is an important part of expressing a sign. With number signs you will notice that palm orientation sometimes changes depending on the context.

1

1 year old

LOCATION

Understanding the location of a sign means that you know where to express the sign in relation to your body. Some signs are made near the chest, while others are made near the forehead or shoulder. Changing the location of a sign can change the meaning.

INTRODUCTION

MOVEMENTS

Because ASL is a visually active language, the most difficult requirement of a sign illustration is to show movement. To fascilitate the three-dimensional nature of signs, illustrations incorporate a number of helpful features.

Arrows show the direction, path, and repetition of the movement. Here are the arrows you will see.

Directional arrows ⇨ point in the direction the sign is to be made. See sign examples below.

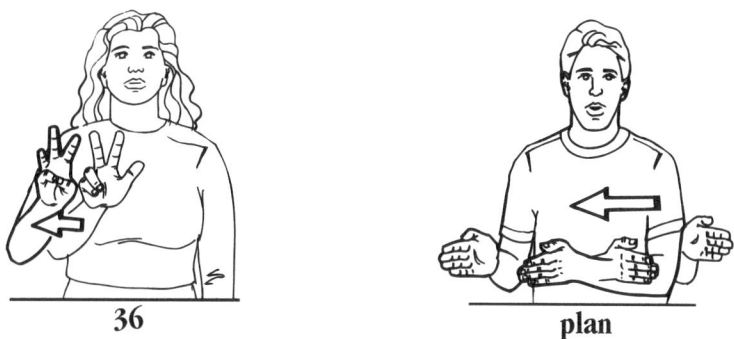

Bi-directional arrows ⇔ indicate a back and forth motion. See sign examples below.

Path arrows ⤳ show you the path of movement of the sign. See sign examples below.

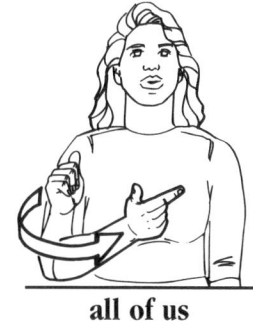

ix

INTRODUCTION

Repetive arrows ⇨ show you the sign's movement is repeated twice or more. See sign examples below.

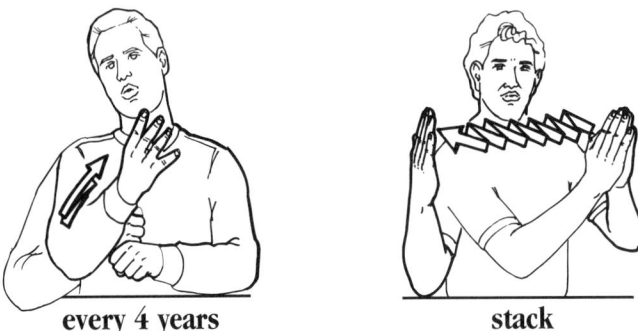

A touch is when part of the handshape touches the chest, shoulder or other part of the body. Touches are shown this way.

Examples of touch marks:

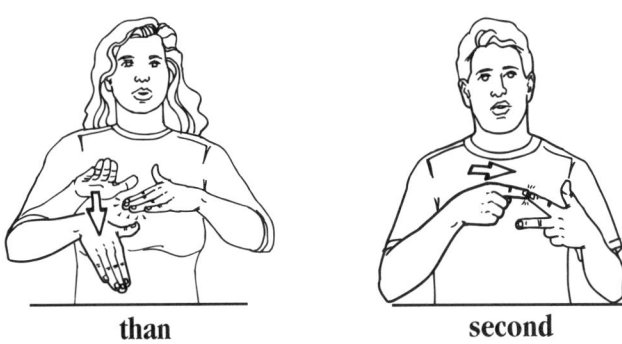

When a handshape is supposed to be "wiggled" or moved back and forth slightly, there will be wiggle marks indicating this.

Examples of wiggle marks:

INTRODUCTION

To illustrate how motion can affect the meaning of a sign, and how the detail of a sign illustration can help you evaluate that motion, look at the following three signs.

As you can see, the handshapes, movements, and locations of these signs are all similar, but the meanings are different.

Some signs begin and end in the same location, while other change location from beginning to end and the sign illustration indicates this. In this book, line thickness is used to distinguish the position of the arms and hands at the beginning of the sign's motion from that at the end of the sign's motion. If the lines of the arms and hands are thin, they indicate the placement of the arms and hands at the beginning of the sign. If, at a different place in the drawing, the lines of the arms and hands are thick, they indicate the placement of the arms and hands at the end of the movement. Here are some examples of signs with movement indicated by line thickness.

If you are able to indentify and evaluate the four parameters of a sign, your ability to use sign illustrations as a learning tool will be increased.

INTRODUCTION

ASL Illustration Conventions

All sign illustrations depict a right-handed signer. Imagine that the person in the illustration is facing you. For a right-handed reader to copy a sign illustration, remember that the hand in the illustration will appear opposite of the way you will need to make the sign. For a left-handed signer, the illustration can be used as a mirror image.

The order in which you read sign illustrations and phrases that have multiple illustrations is very important. Words or phrases that contain multiple illustrations need to be read illustration by illustration from left to right. Individual illustrations then need to be read according to the direction or movement of the sign shown.

The following examples show vocabulary with multiple illustrations.

1 yard   3,535

HOW TO USE THE DVD

The chapters and sections of this book are set up to coincide with the topics and order of the companion DVD *Number Signs for Everyone*. Although the signs included here and in the DVD are not identical, the content is similar. This book and the companion DVD have been designed to reinforce each other, and both have special features and capabilities that are unique and valuable to the learning process.

A final note to the reader. ASL is a dynamic, ever growing and changing language. The signs you see in this book are intended to give a person learning ASL basic information about the number sign system. In the signing community, you will see other variations of number signs, but, after studying the illustrations here, you will be well on your way to mastering numbers and their use in context in ASL.

CHAPTER 1
HOW MANY

CARDINAL numbers are used to describe quantities: 1 shoe, 2 trees, 3 lbs of flour. ASL uses cardinal numbers for counting and expressing quantities. The ASL number system is based on whole numbers in units of 10.

NUMBERS 0–10

1.1

Zero, and the basic signs for counting from 1 to 10 are shown here (note that numbers 1 through 5 have the palm facing inward toward the signer; 0, and 6 through 9 have the palm facing outward).

CHAPTER 1

1.2 NUMBERS 11–30

The following signs are for numbers 11 through 30. Note the variations in palm orientation here. The signs for 16 through 19 begin with the 10 handshape, and end with the hand twisting outward to form the sign for 6, 7, 8, or 9. The signs for 20 through 29, except 22, use a different handshape, an L-handshape to represent 2.

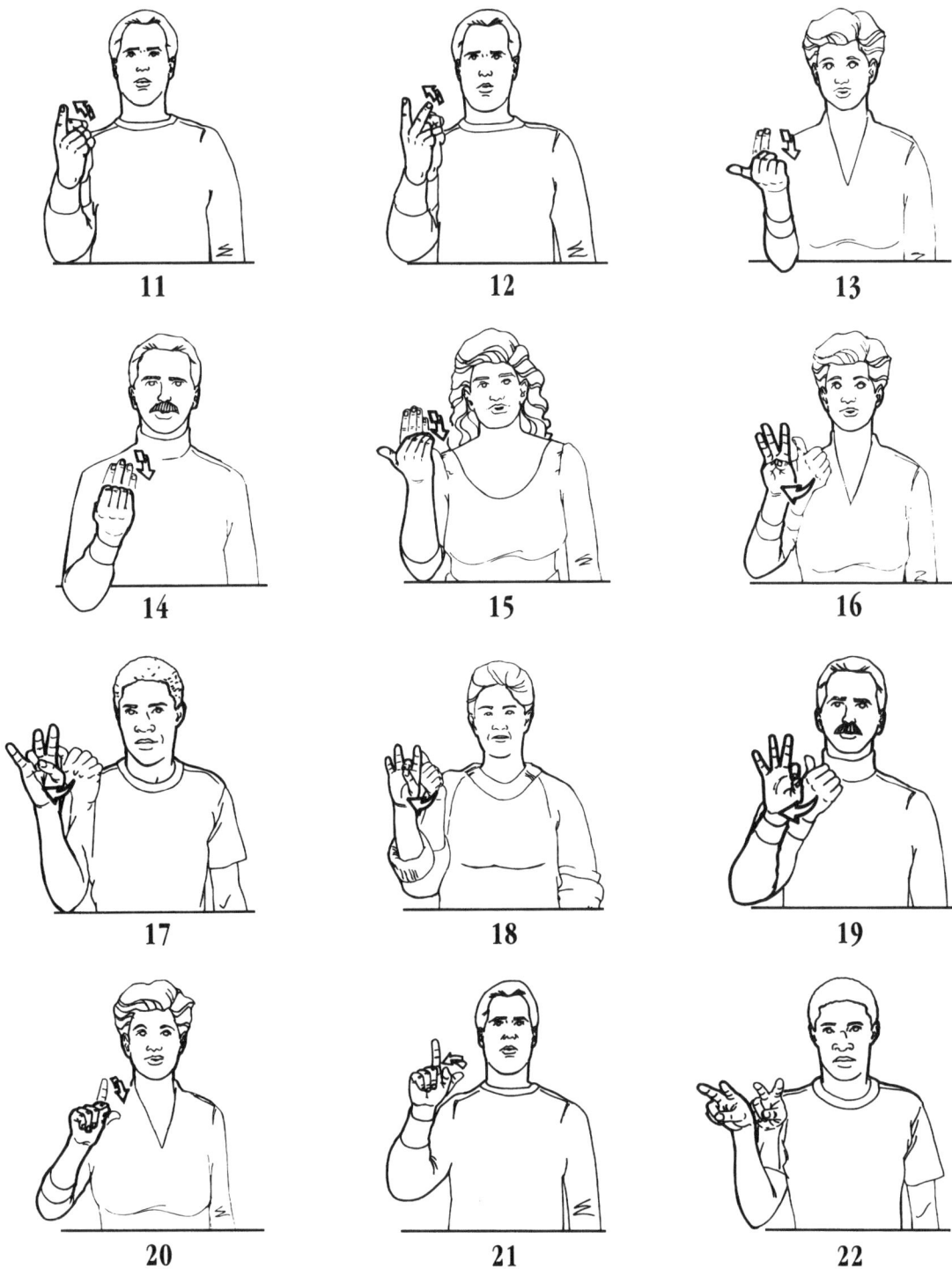

HOW MANY

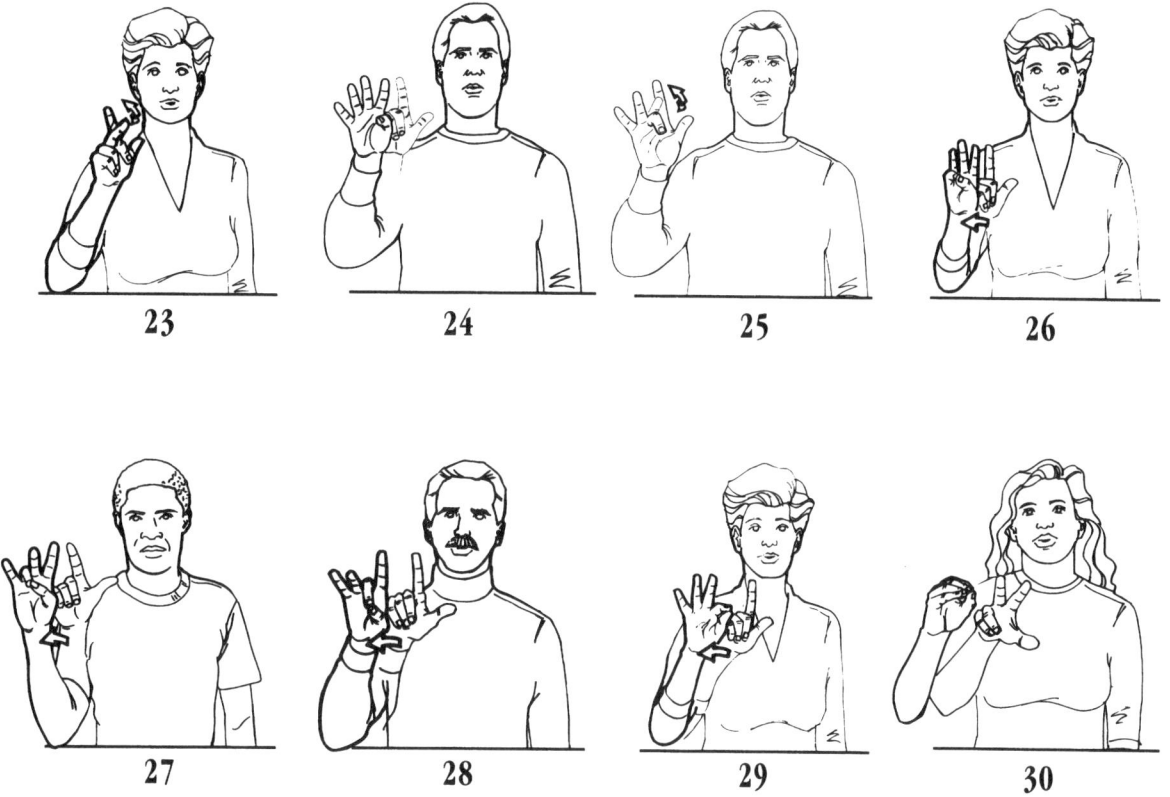

NUMBERS 31–109, AND MULTIPLES OF 100

1.3

This section presents sign illustrations for numbers 31 through 109. Special attention should be paid to multiples of 11 (22, 33, 44, etc.). When these numbers are signed, the same number is repeated, with the handshape bouncing twice. Another unique group of signs comprises two-digit combinations using the numbers 6, 7, 8, and 9 (such as 68, 76, or 97). The signs have a twisting movement to emphasize and clarify the position of the thumb as it shifts from one fingertip to the other, creating the number combination required. Notice the numbers 101-109 are handled so the 0 is clearly shown. Additionally, illustrations for 200, 300, and 400 through 900 are shown.

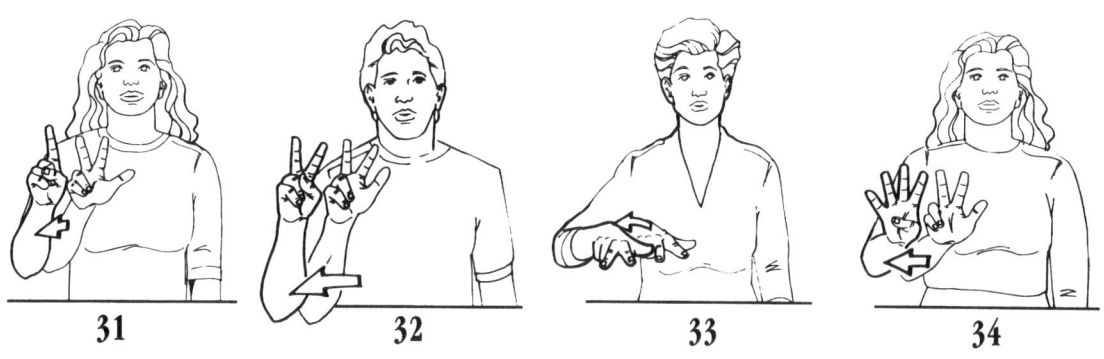

CHAPTER 1

HOW MANY

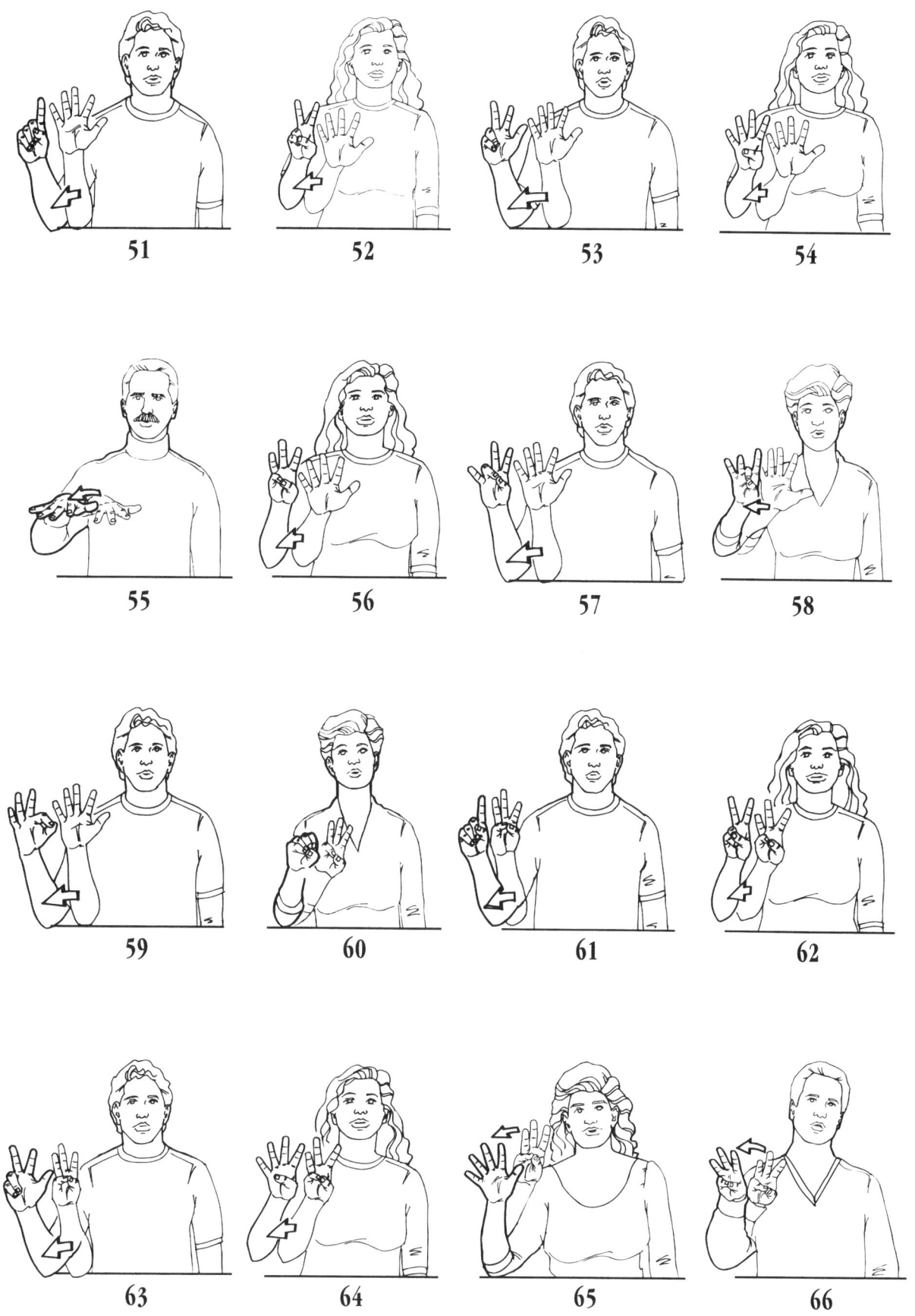

Chapter 1

HOW MANY

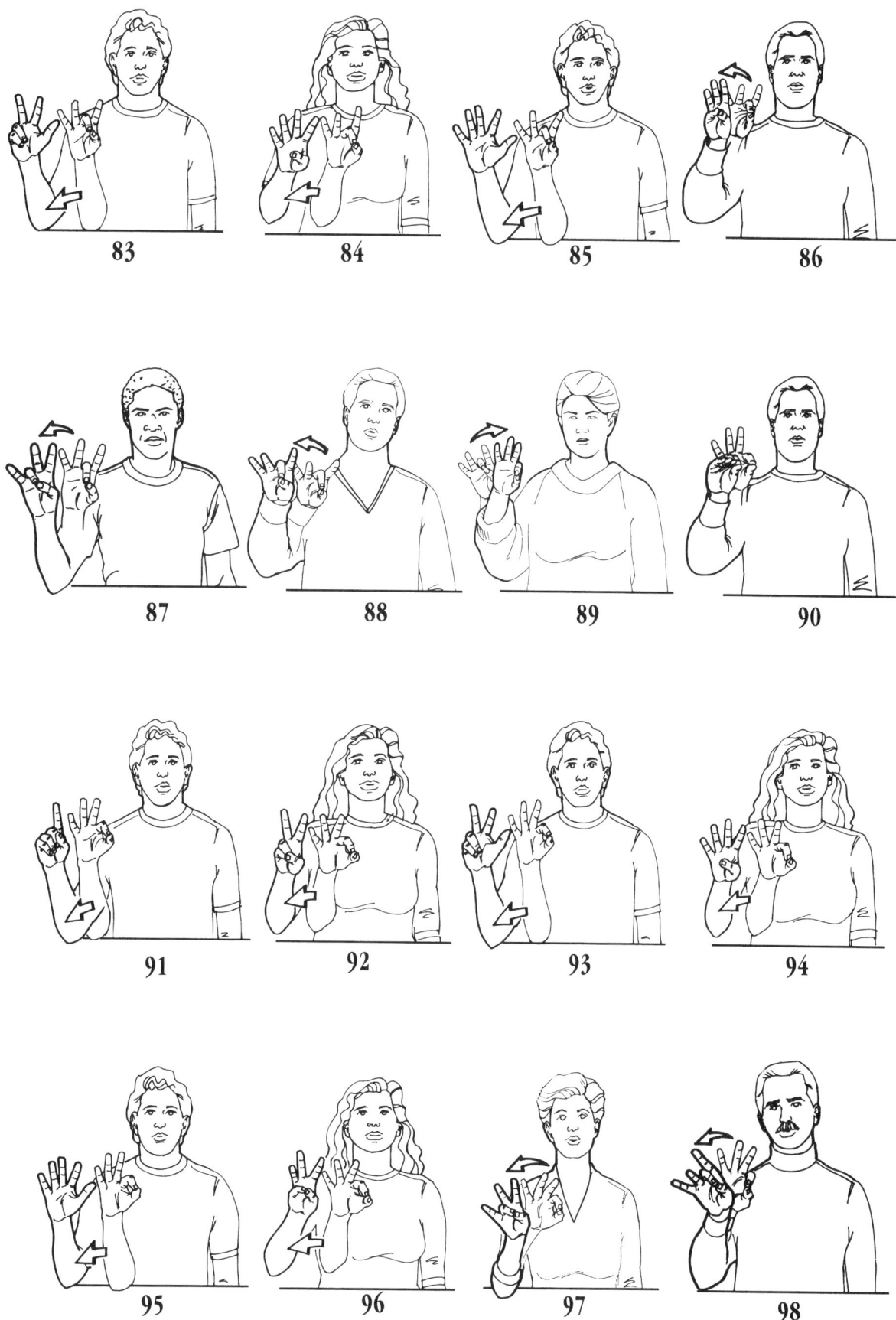

Chapter 1

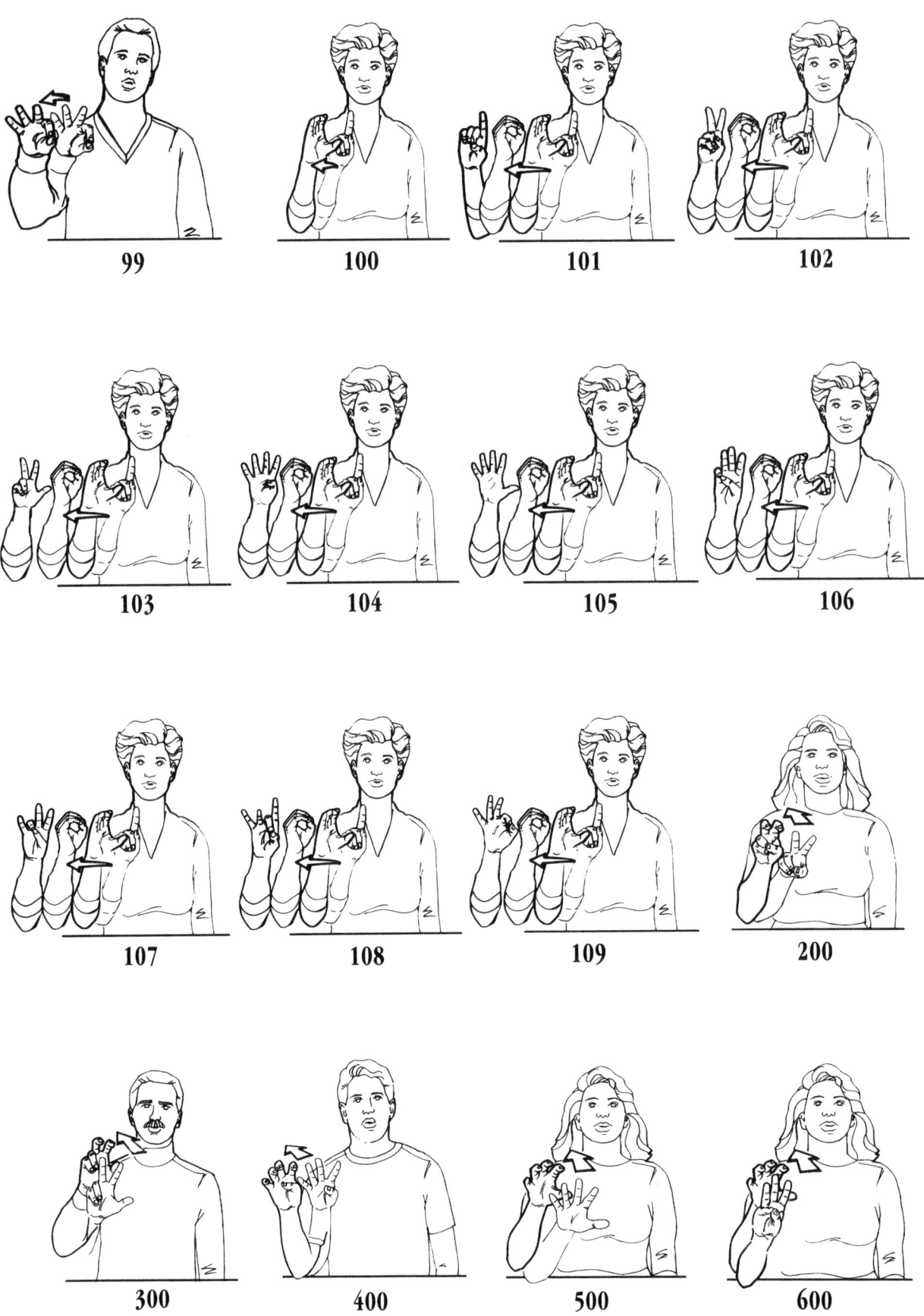

700

800

900

EMPHASIS

1.4

Number signs include emphasis, which adds context to ASL sentences by showing whether the person signing feels the quantity they are discussing is normal or exceptional. The following illustrations use a sharp singular motion and facial expressions to show emphasis. In ASL, sign formations often lose repetition of movement when they are emphasized.

200

300

400

500

LARGE NUMBERS AND MIXED NUMBERS

1.5

Here illustrations of larger numbers, such as 1,000 to 1 billion, and mixed numbers are shown. Mixed numbers are signed in parts as in three hundred, sixty-five, not three, six, five.

1,000

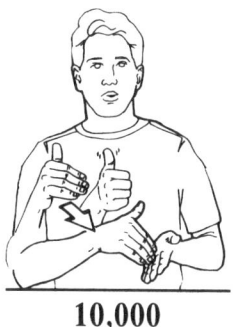
10,000

50,000

Chapter 1

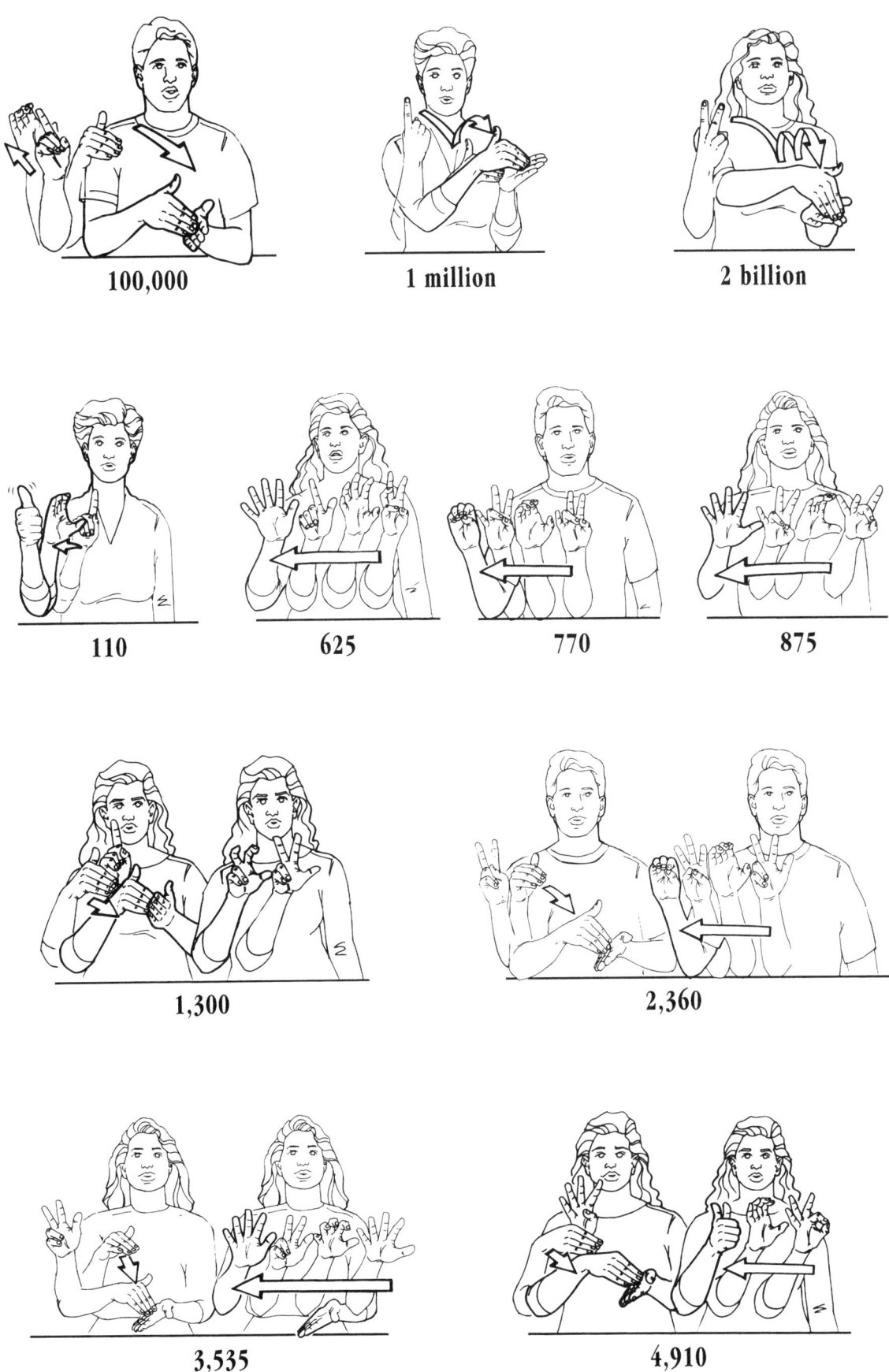

HOW MANY

APPROXIMATIONS

1.6

Sometimes it is useful or necessary to express an approximate number. There are several ways of doing this in ASL. One is to sign the number, but add a facial expression indicating that you are not sure of the exact amount. Another is to add a sign indicating that you are estimating, or add a wiggling motion.

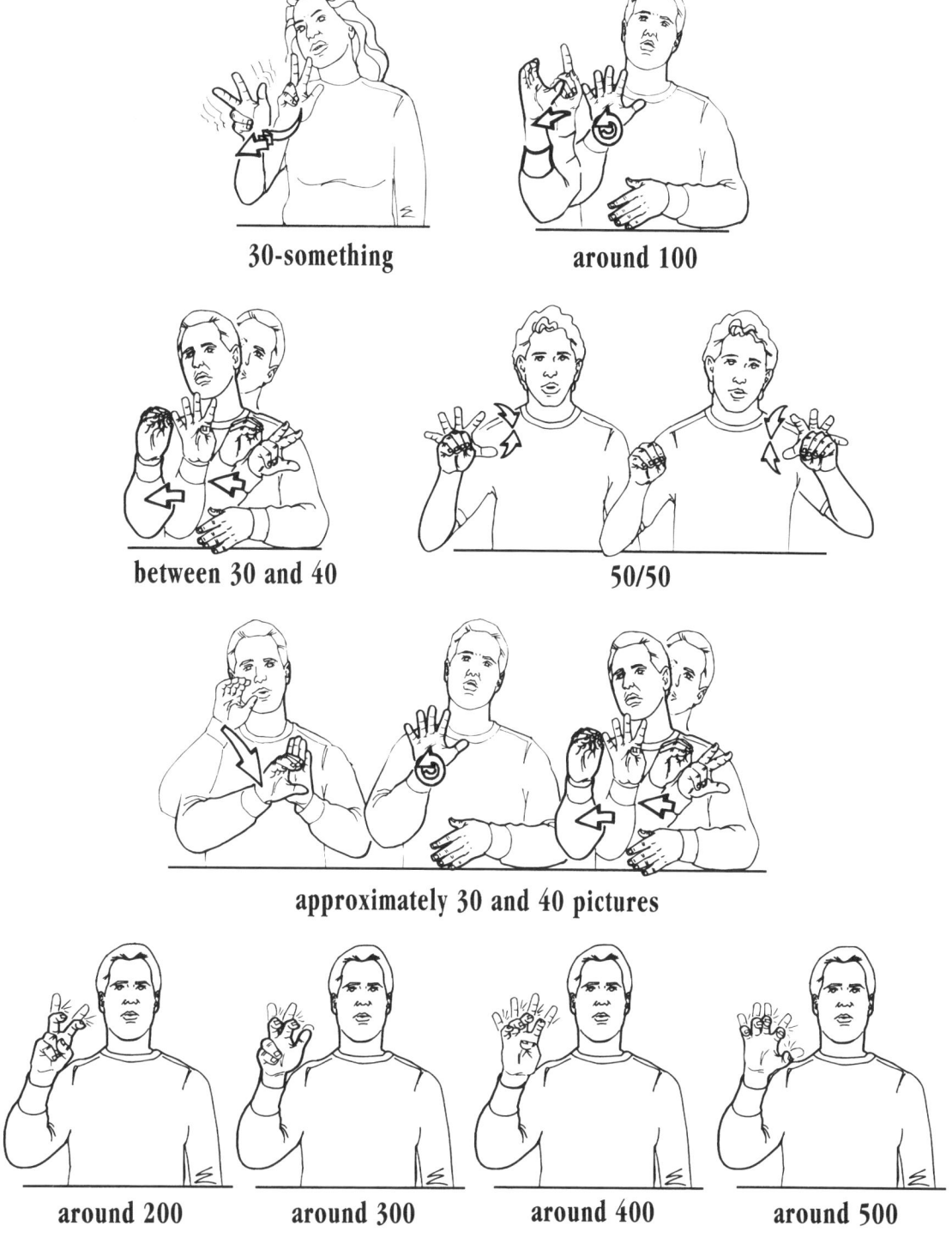

1.7 Number Representation

Number representation is an important part of ASL structure. These signs use a number handshape with modified motion or location, or a noun to express a meaning.

| number of baby teeth | double date | 4 couples together |

| 1 person moving | 1 person approaching 2 people | 5 people approaching |

| 2 of us | 2 of them | 3 of us |

| 4 of us | 5 of you | 6 of us | all of us |

HOW MANY

QUANTIFIERS

1.8

So far, we have been using numbers to express absolute quantities, that is, amounts that can be understood correctly out of context. In addition to absolute numbers, ASL has another kind of sign for showing quantity using quantifiers. Quantifiers represent attributes of things in a relative sense, rather than discussing exact amounts with whole numbers. Words like many, more, and few are examples of generic quantifiers.

any · all · all · most

many · some · few · none

list · hordes · traffic · pile

stack · crowd · all kinds/variety · nothing left

13

CHAPTER 1

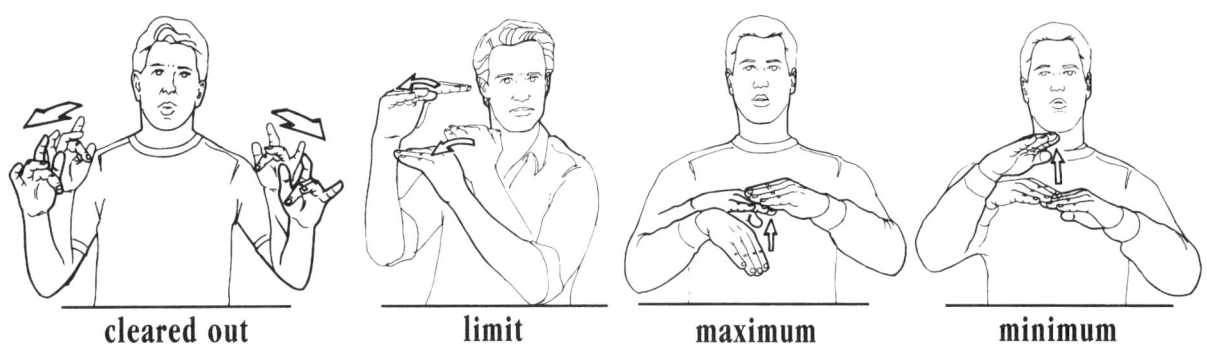

cleared out   limit   maximum   minimum

Phrases using Quantifiers

How many?

Thirty people came.

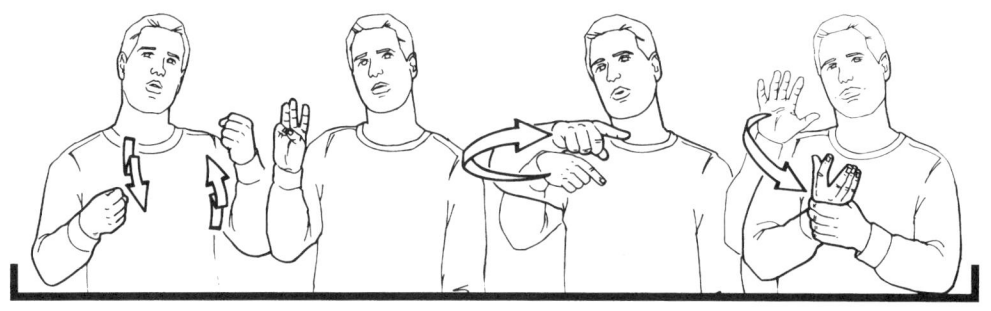

Six people are in the car.

HOW MANY

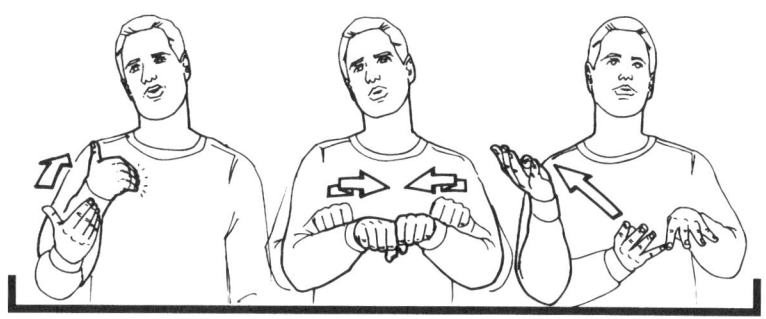

I have rows of shoes.

I gave a book to both of you.

I assume 2 cars left, one following the other.

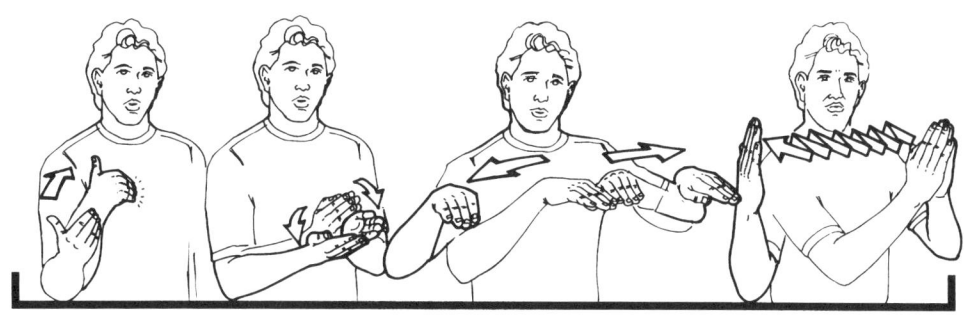

I have a whole shelf of books.

CHAPTER 1

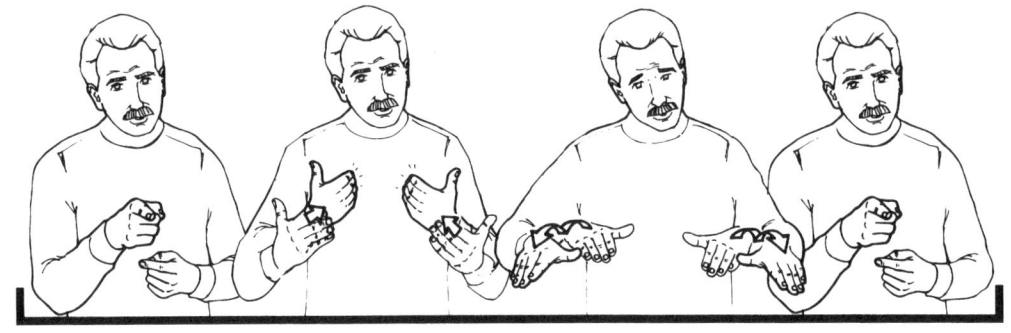

Do you have children?

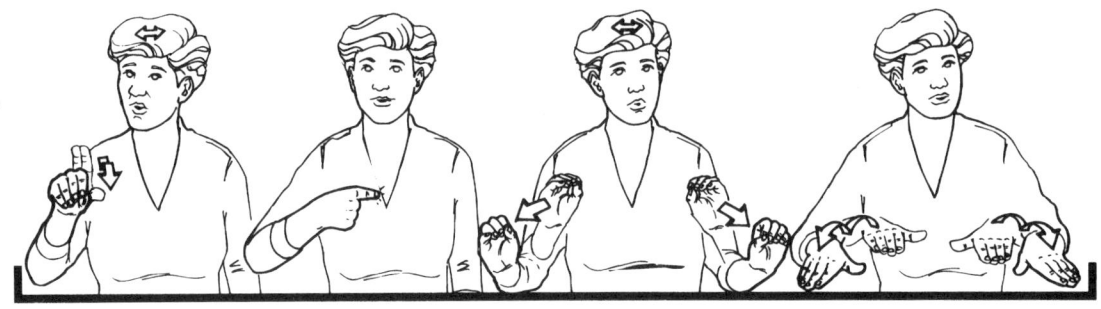

No, I don't have any children.

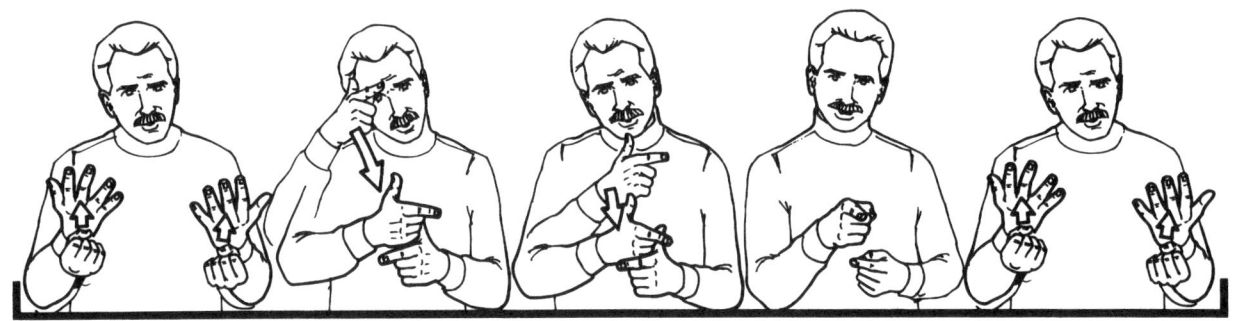

How many brothers and sisters do you have?

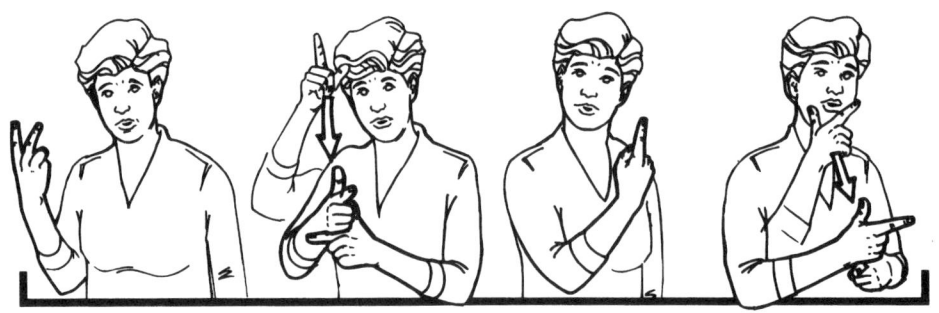

I have 2 brothers and 1 sister.

CHAPTER 2
MONEY

MONEY is a part of everyday life. The following examples of number signs for monetary values show the basic signs for dollars and cents and show phrases using money signs.

CENTS

2.1

Cents are the smallest monetary value in ASL. The following are various quantities of cents. Notice that 25 cents uses a common variation of the number 25.

1¢   3¢   5¢

10¢   15¢   20¢   25¢

50¢   55¢   60¢

17

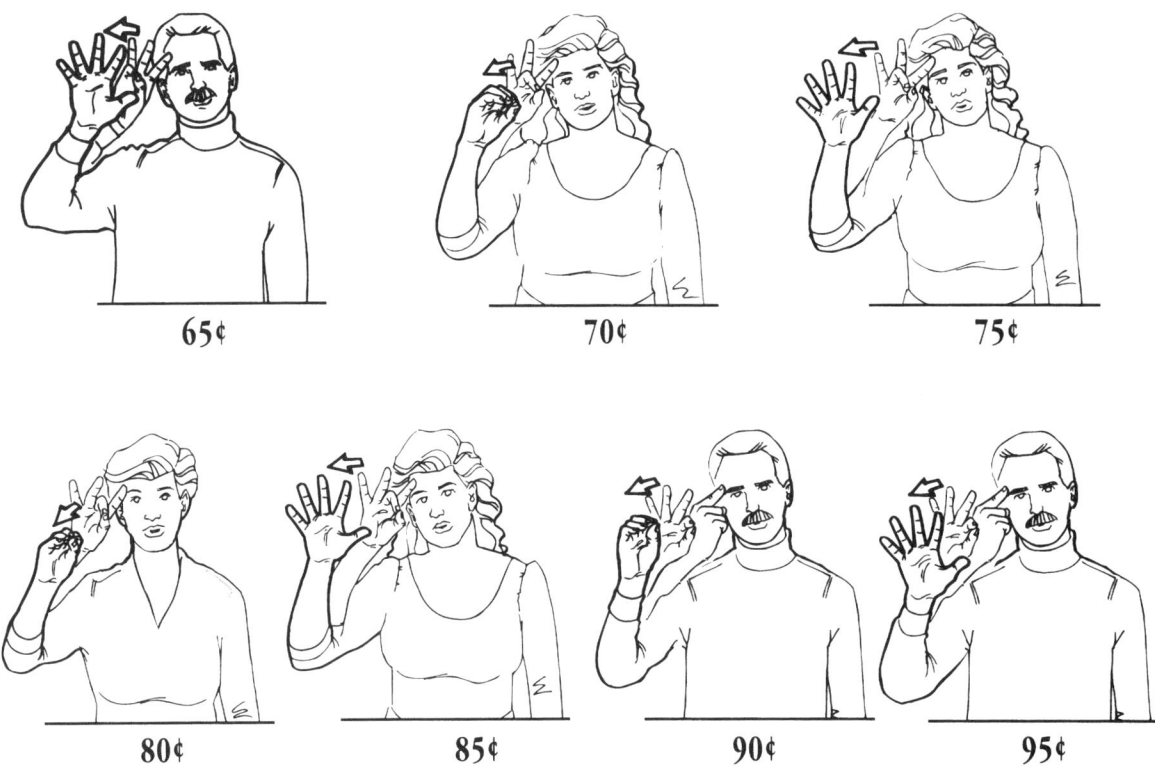

2.2 Fingerspelling cents

You can also sign a number and fingerspell the word *"C-E-N-T-S"* to show the amount. Remember, if the amount is a number from 1 to 5, you sign the number with your palm facing toward your body, and then turn your hand palm-outward to fingerspell *cents*.

DOLLARS

Following are various signs for dollar values. With dollar numbers 1 through 9 you do not separate the number and dollar sign; you use the number handshape with a twisting motion to indicate dollars. For numbers 10 or greater the signs change. The signs for numbers and dollars are separated.

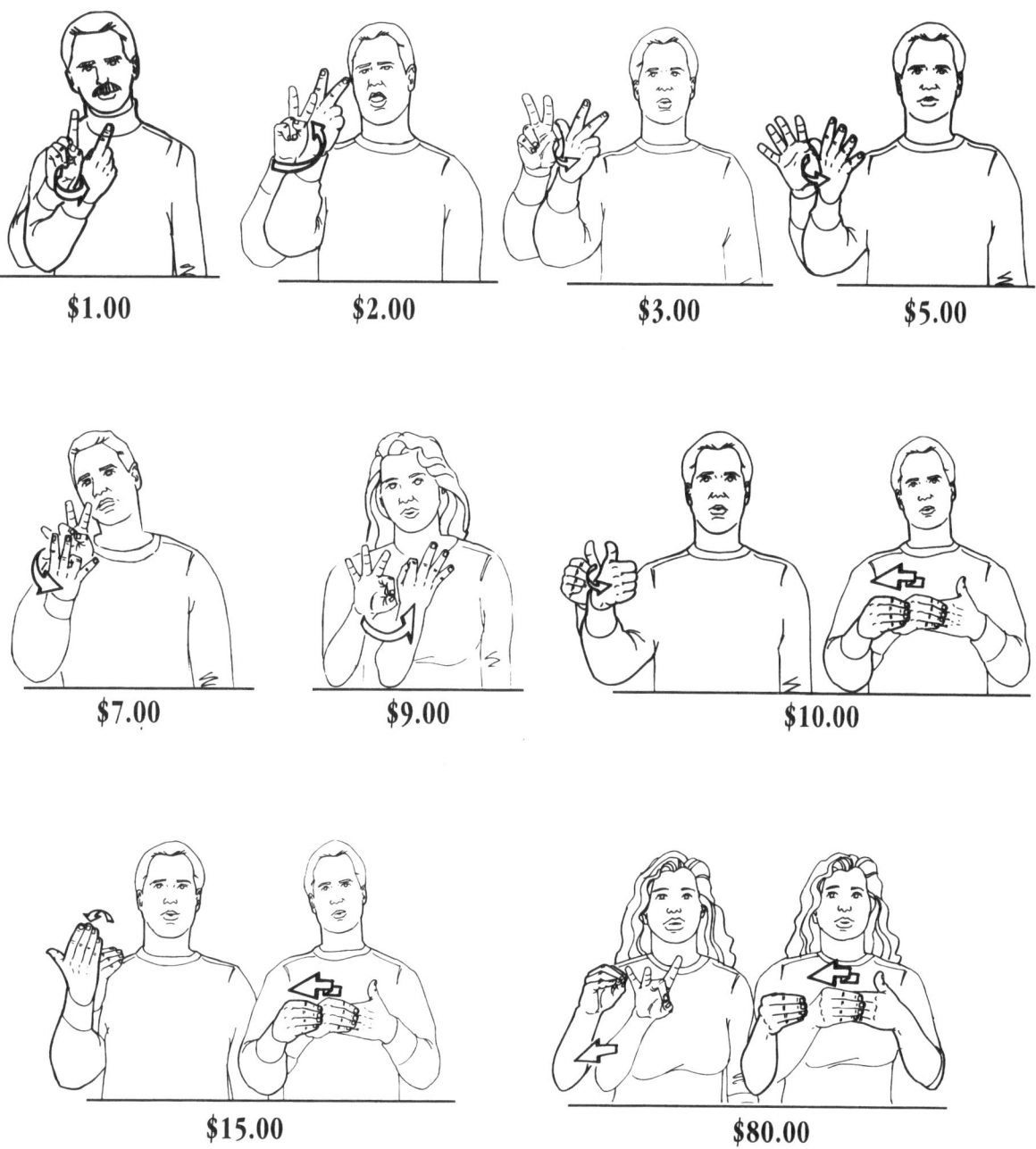

CHAPTER 2

2.4 MIXED MONEY SIGNS

The previous rules for signing dollars and cents apply to mixed monetary values such as $10.25. In English, people may say "ten twenty-five" when discussing cost. For mixed money signs in ASL with 10 dollars or greater, the signs for dollars and sign for cents are sometimes lost when incorporated in a sentence. The samples below show mixed money signs.

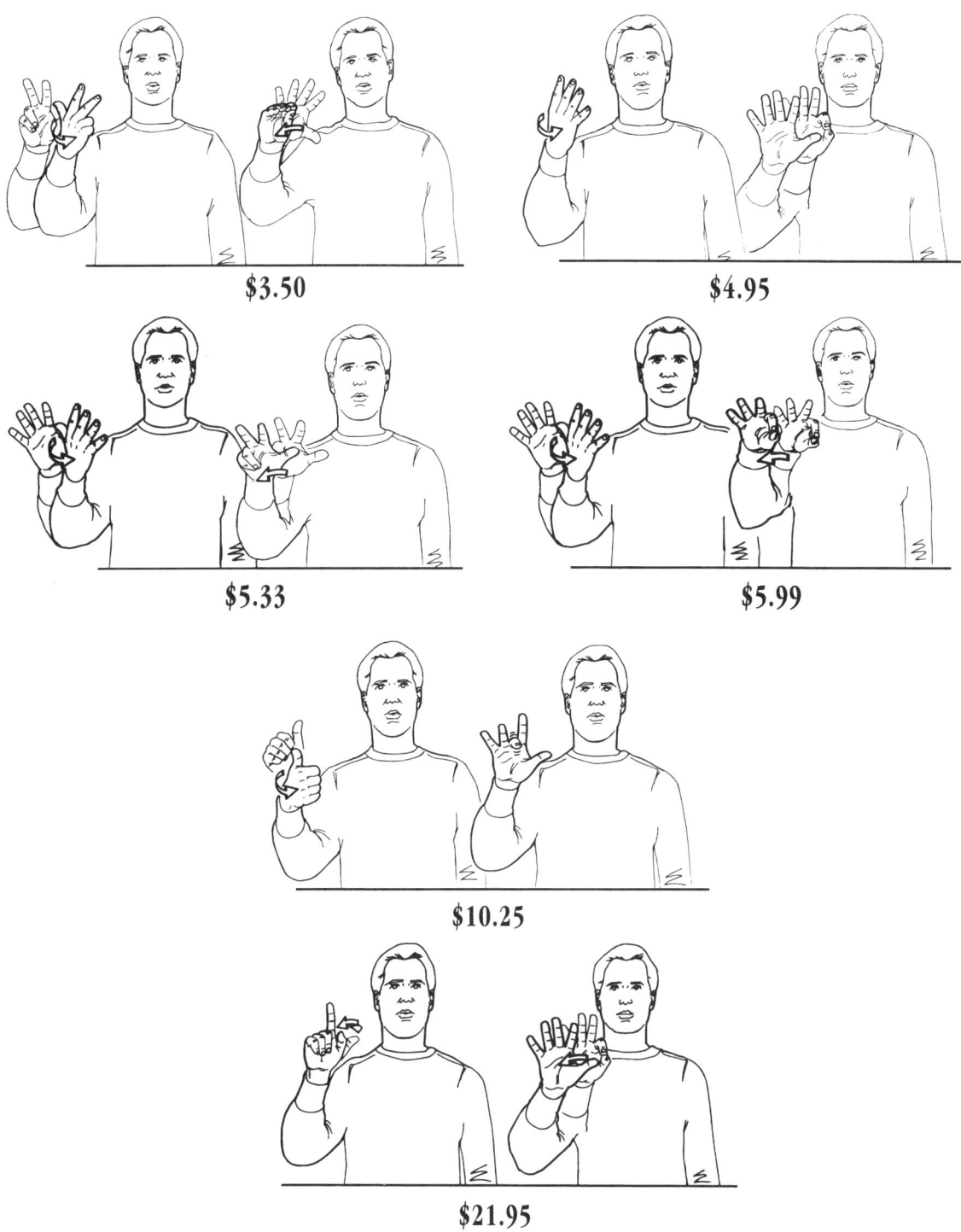

$3.50

$4.95

$5.33

$5.99

$10.25

$21.95

APPROXIMATE MONEY SIGNS

MONEY

2.5

Sometimes, we do not know, or it is not important, exactly how many cents are involved. The next sign shows how to approximate a monetary value.

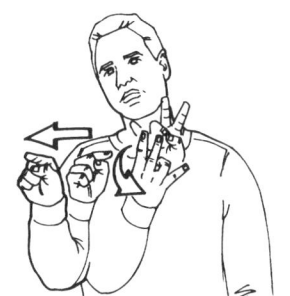

7 dollars and some odd cents

Phrases Using Money Signs

How much?

How much?

How much is the admission fee?

It's $3.00.

Chapter 2

How much is the camera worth?

It's nice . . . it's worth 80 dollars and 46 c-e-n-t-s.

It's cheap! It costs $9.05 plus tax.

CHAPTER 3
FINANCES

THIS chapter focuses on vocabulary related to money. Examples of phrases using the vocabulary in the proper context are given.

PAYMENT AND SPENDING

3.1

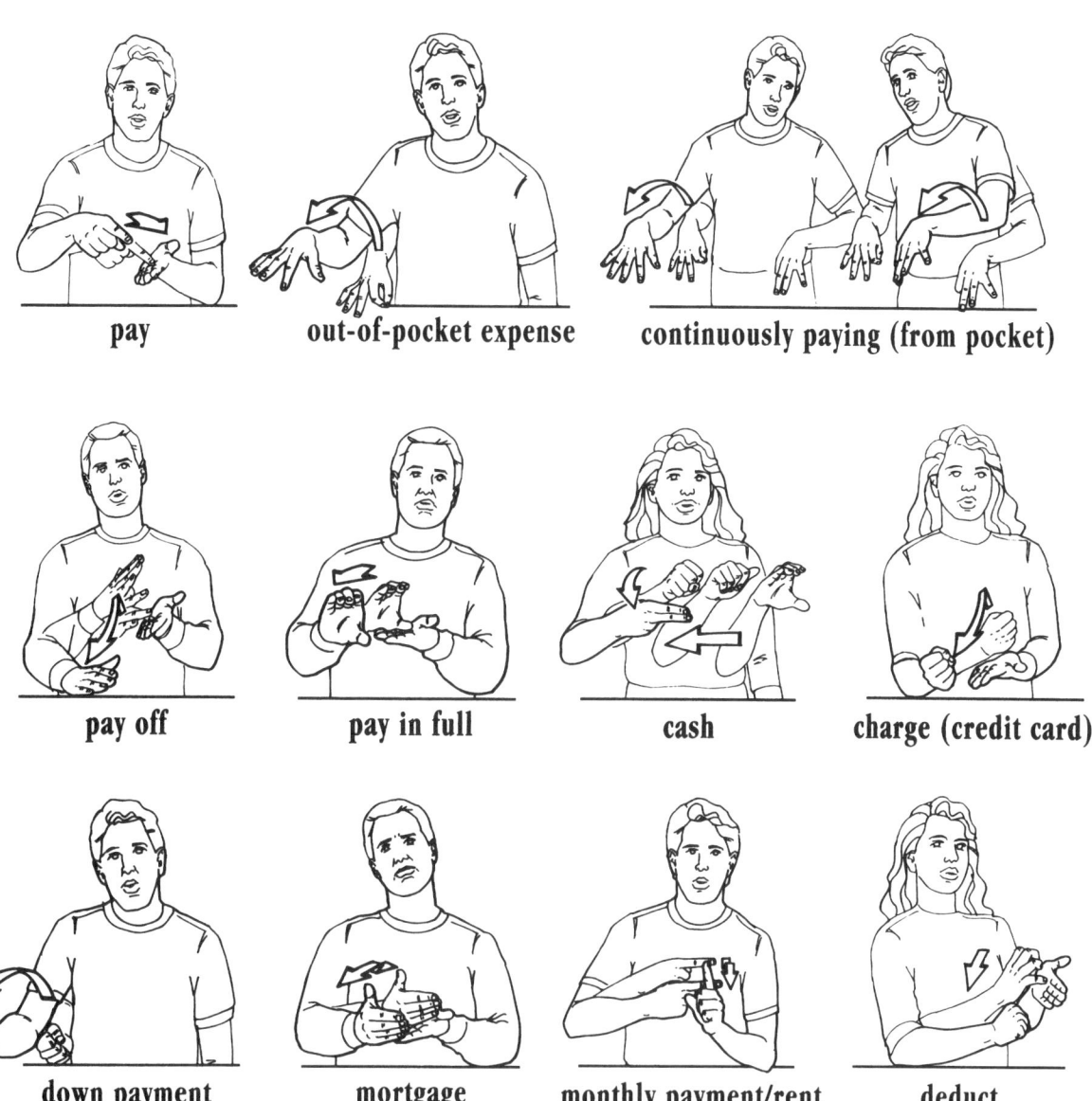

pay out-of-pocket expense continuously paying (from pocket)

pay off pay in full cash charge (credit card)

down payment mortgage monthly payment/rent deduct

23

Chapter 3

Phrases Using Payment Signs

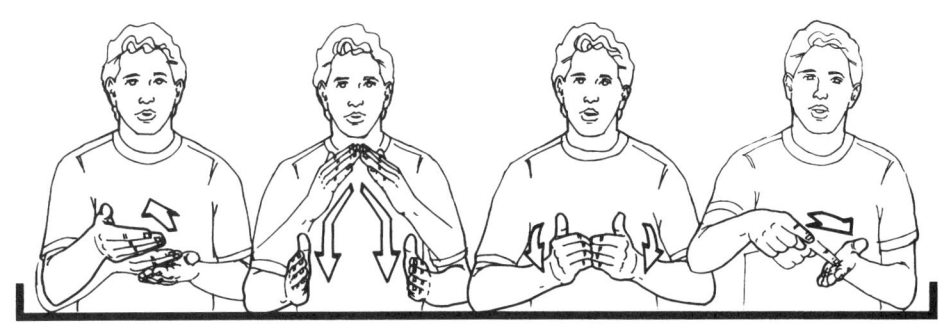

How did you pay for the house you bought?

I paid in full!

INCOME

FINANCES

3.2

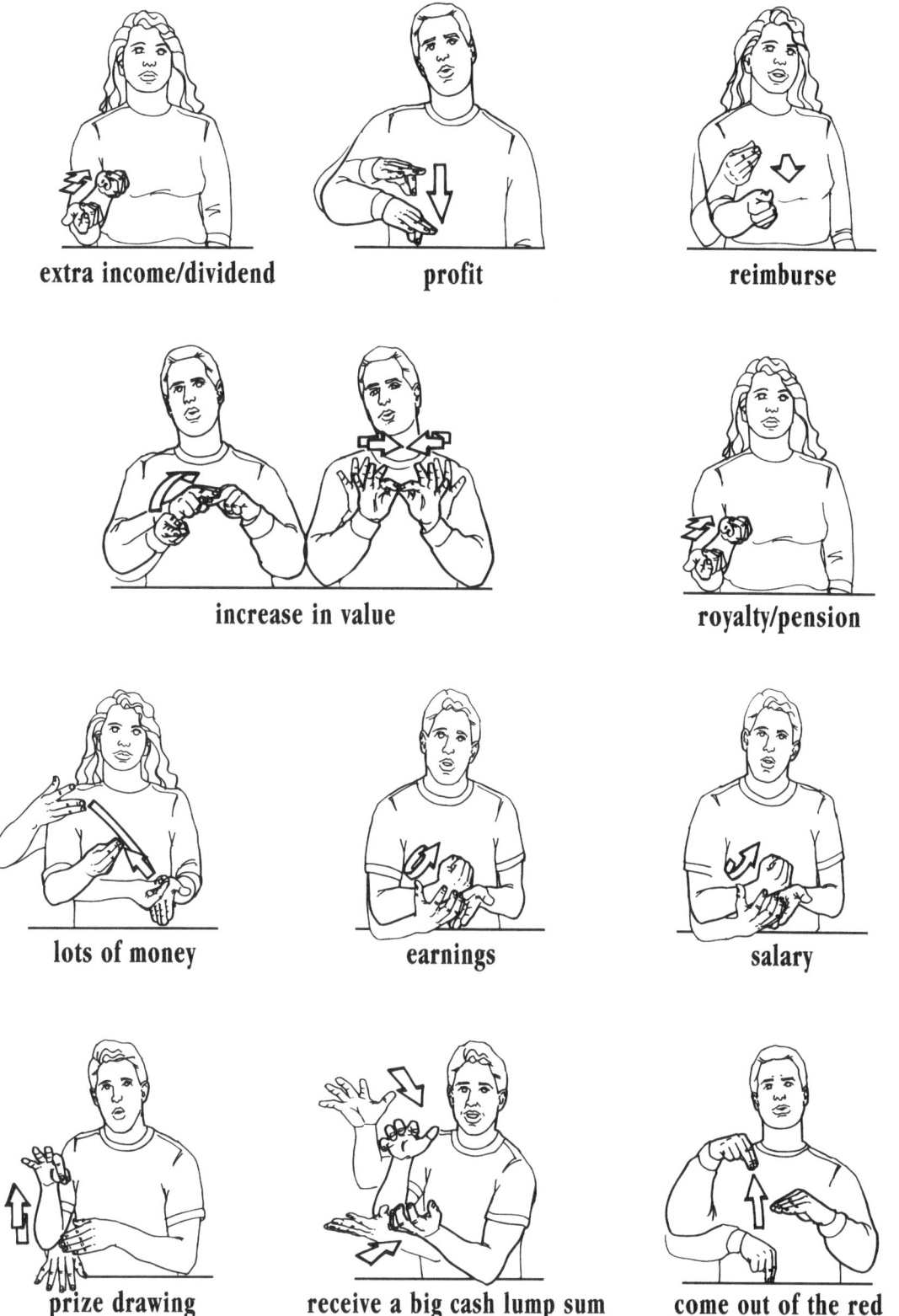

extra income/dividend · profit · reimburse

increase in value · royalty/pension

lots of money · earnings · salary

prize drawing · receive a big cash lump sum · come out of the red

CHAPTER 3

Phrases Using Income Signs

Does your job pay well?

I make good money!

3.3 LOSSES

FINANCES

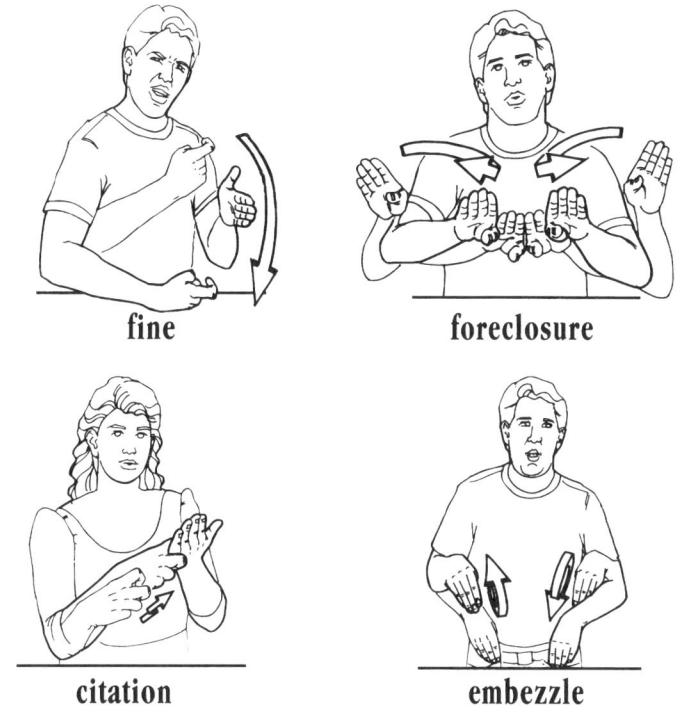

FINANCE-RELATED SIGNS

3.4

Chapter 3

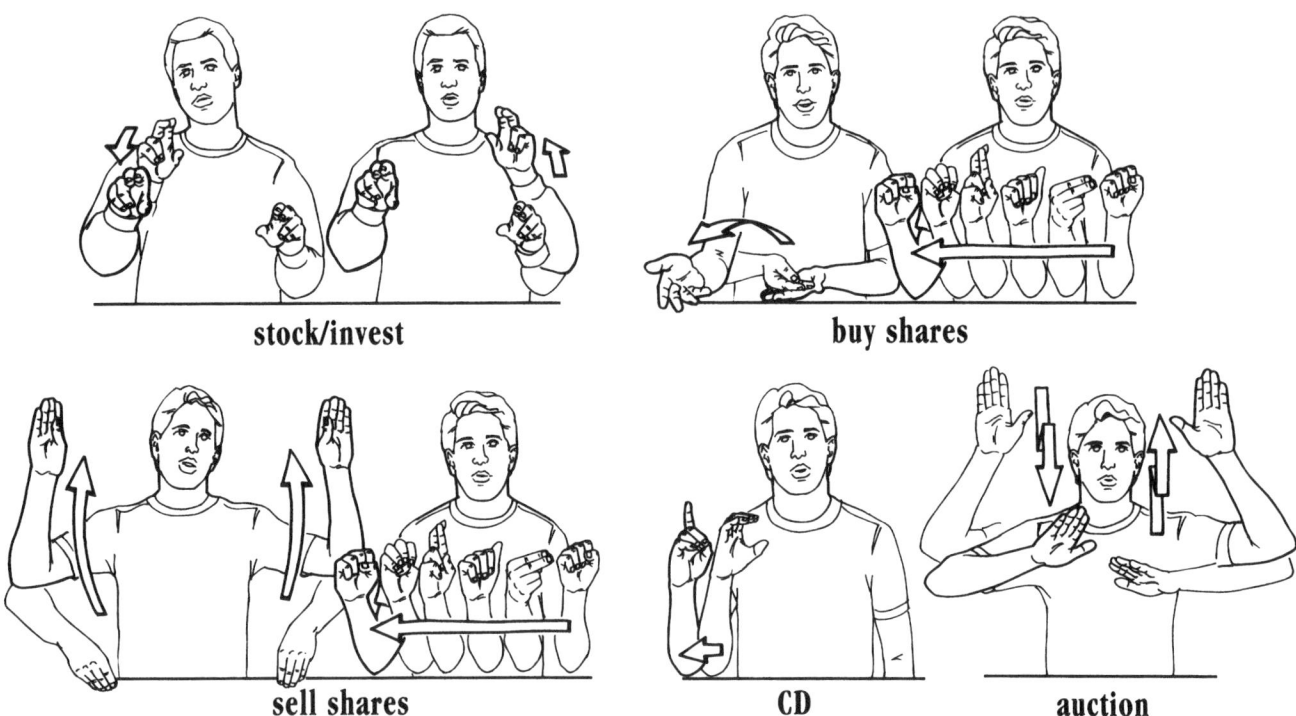

stock/invest   buy shares

sell shares   CD   auction

Phrases Using Finance-Related Signs

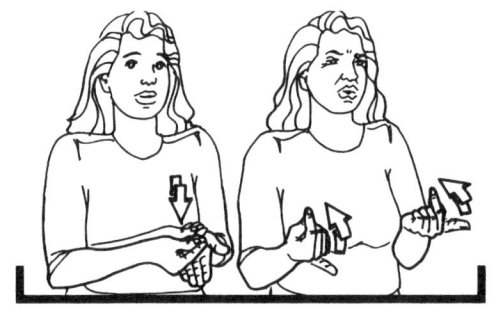

What do you do with your money?

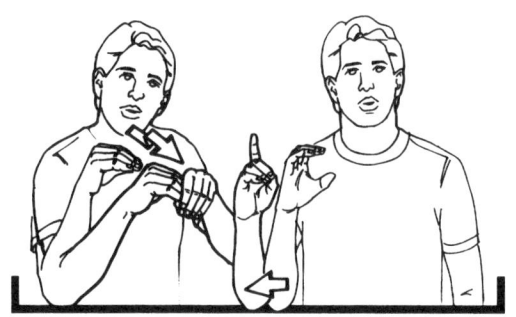

Put it in my savings or CD's.

FINANCE-RELATED OCCUPATIONS

Most of the signs in this next group are compounds of a verb sign for the activity plus a sign that is often translated as "-er" to indicate that an occupation is being discussed.

Chapter 3

financial planner

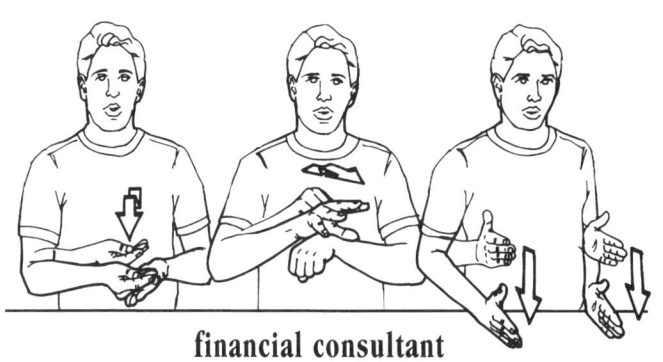
financial consultant

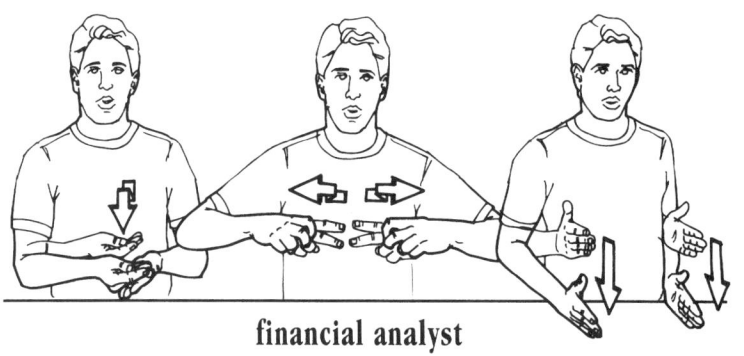
financial analyst

CHAPTER 4
MEASUREMENTS

NUMBERS are not only used for counting, but also for measuring, comparing, and otherwise commenting on quantity. This chapter shows number signs that give information about "how much" and "how many."

NUMERICAL SIGNS SHOWING QUANTITY AND FREQUENCY

4.1

ASL has a common pattern from once all the way up to five times, using the corresponding handshape for the numbers 1 to 5. Notice in the following sign illustrations how the different numeric handshapes use different fingertips in contact with the base hand to begin the sign.

twice/double   3 times/triple   4 times/quadruple

5 times/quintuple   10 times   1 more

1 more   2 more   2 more

CHAPTER 4

3 more

3 more

Phrase Using Quantity and Frequency Signs

It's 10 times more, Wow!

4.2 QUANTIFIERS

As seen in Chapter 1, Section 8, a quantifier is a word like "all" or "some" that indicates the quantity of something without using an absolute number. The following signs are quantifiers that specifically discuss measurement.

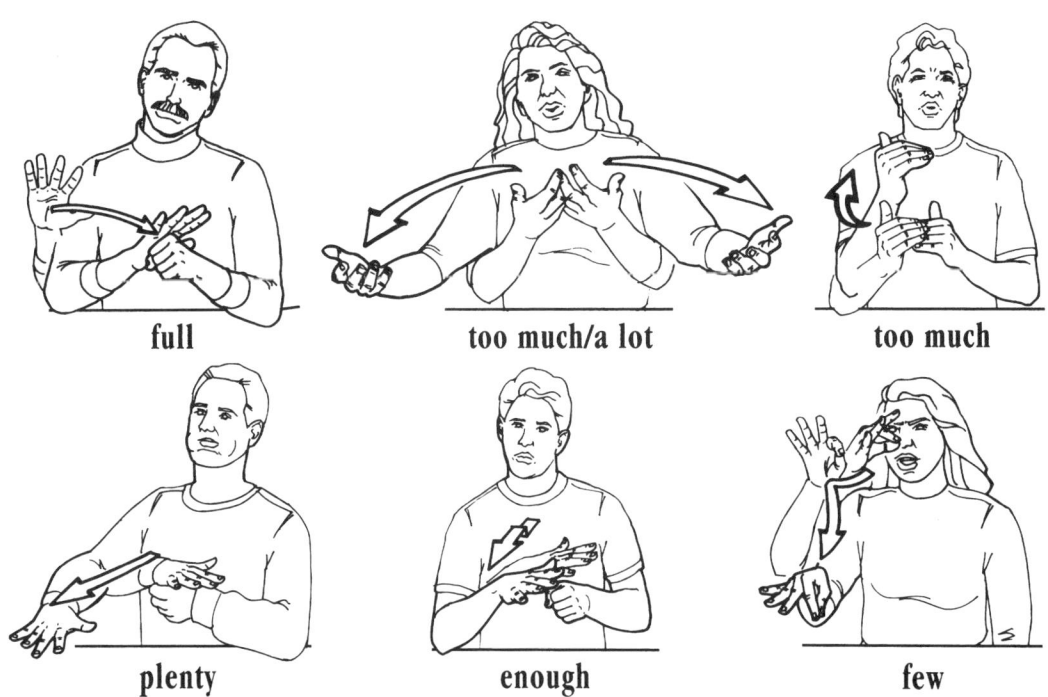

full   too much/a lot   too much

plenty   enough   few

MEASUREMENTS

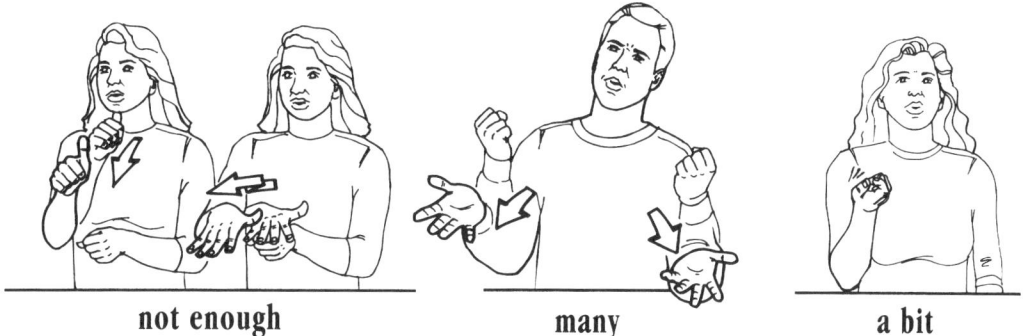

Phrases Using Quantifier Signs

FRACTIONS

4.3

ASL uses space to indicate a fraction, signing the upper number (the numerator), and then dropping the hand slightly and signing the lower number (the denominator). Fractions where both the numerator and the denominator are single digits, for example, *1/2, 1/3, 1/4,* and up to *3/9, 4/9,* and *5/9* are made with the palm facing in toward the signer for both digits. Here are some common fractions.

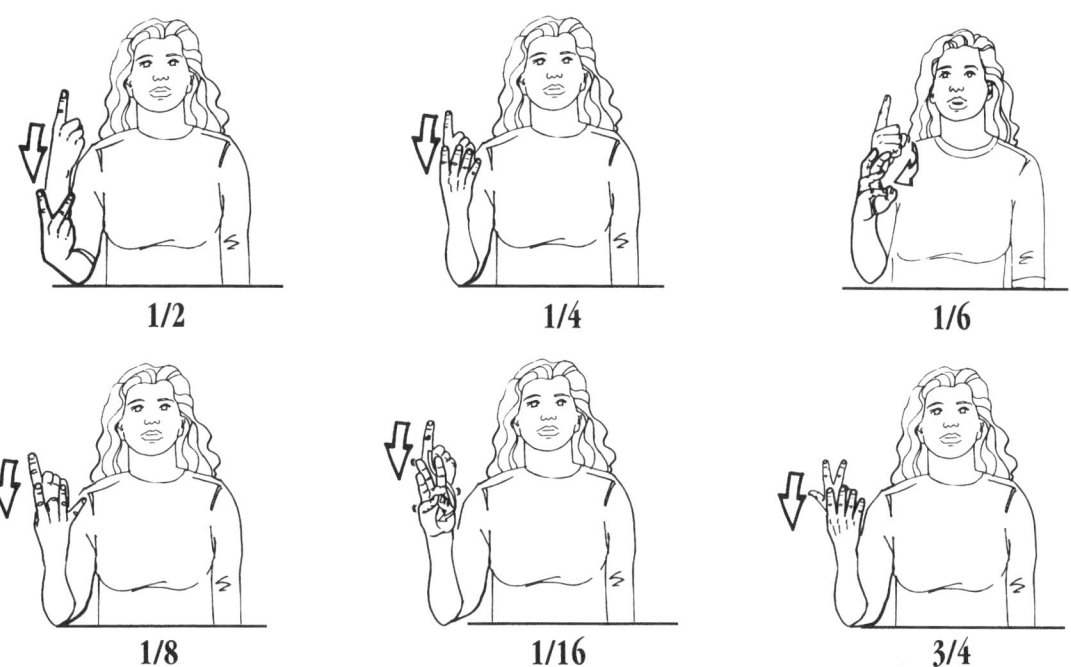

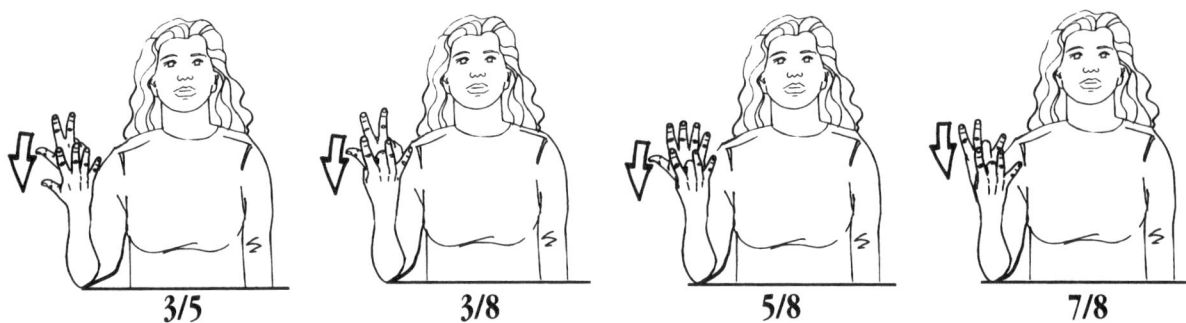

| 3/5 | 3/8 | 5/8 | 7/8 |

Half

Following are signs for *half*. One follows the simple pattern described previously to make the fraction 1/2. The second shows a two-handed sign, translated as "1/2 for you, and 1/2 for me." The third is a special sign based on the verb *cut in half* and does not incorporate any numbers.

| 1/2 |  1/2 for you, 1/2 for me |  half/split |

| half and half |  50/50 |

half French, half Italian

BODY MEASUREMENTS

4.4

Height and other body measurements such as dress size are shown here. One important note in expressing a person's height in ASL is that the numbers are signed with the palm facing toward the signer. As the handshape changes from expressing number of feet to number of inches, the hand moves sharply in the direction of the thumb-side of the hand (that is, to the right if you are right-handed and to the left if you are left-handed).

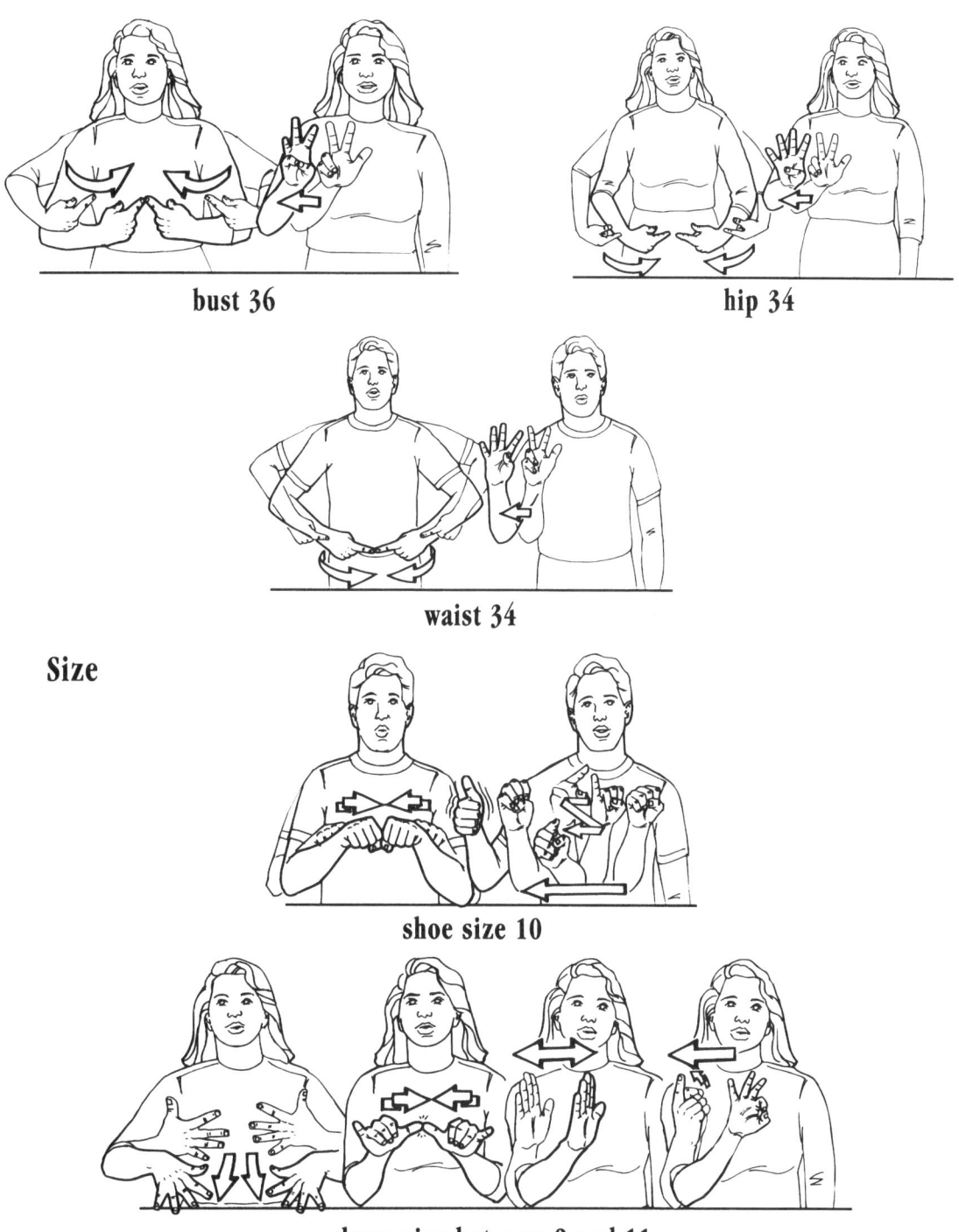

bust 36

hip 34

waist 34

Size

shoe size 10

dress size between 9 and 11

Height

4'11" 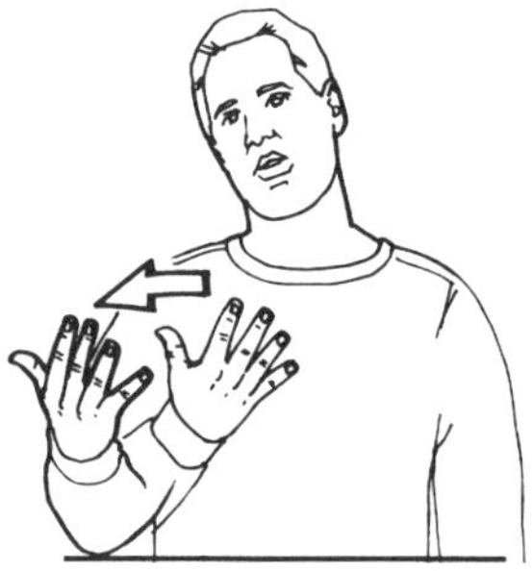   5'5"    6'8"

short    medium 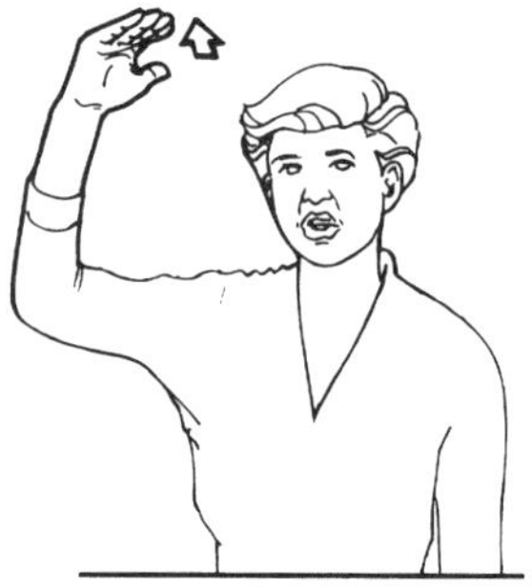   tall

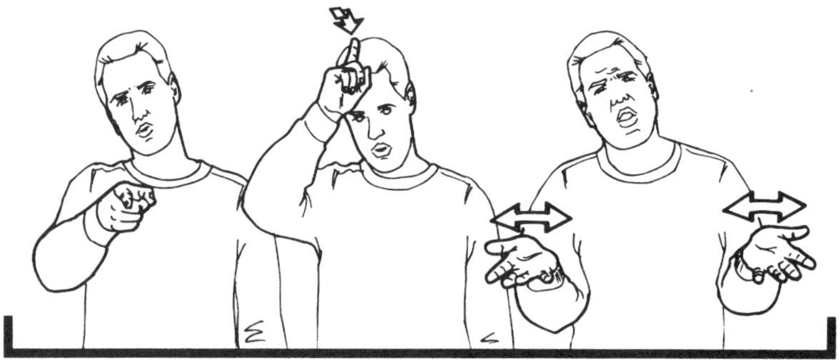

What is your height?

Other Measurements

Length, volume, weight, and temperature are expressed as a counting number or a fraction, followed by the unit of measurement. The units of measurement are most often fingerspelled abbreviations of the English equivalents, rather than sign translations. For example, "one foot" is signed *1 ft*, rather than *1 foot*.

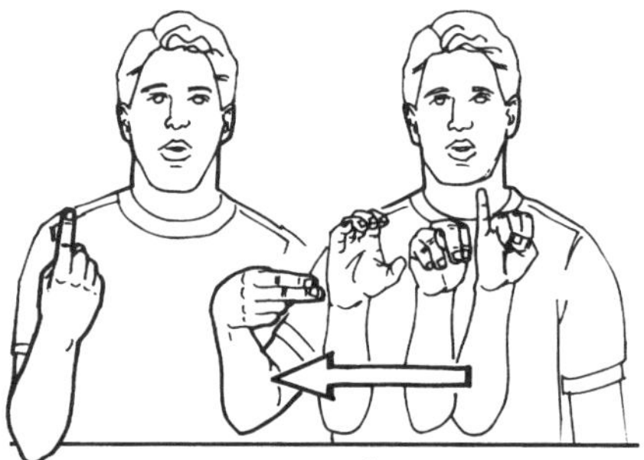

1 inch 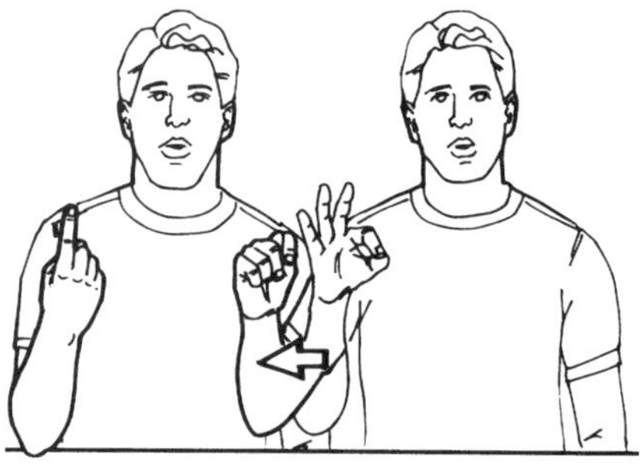   1 foot

MEASUREMENTS

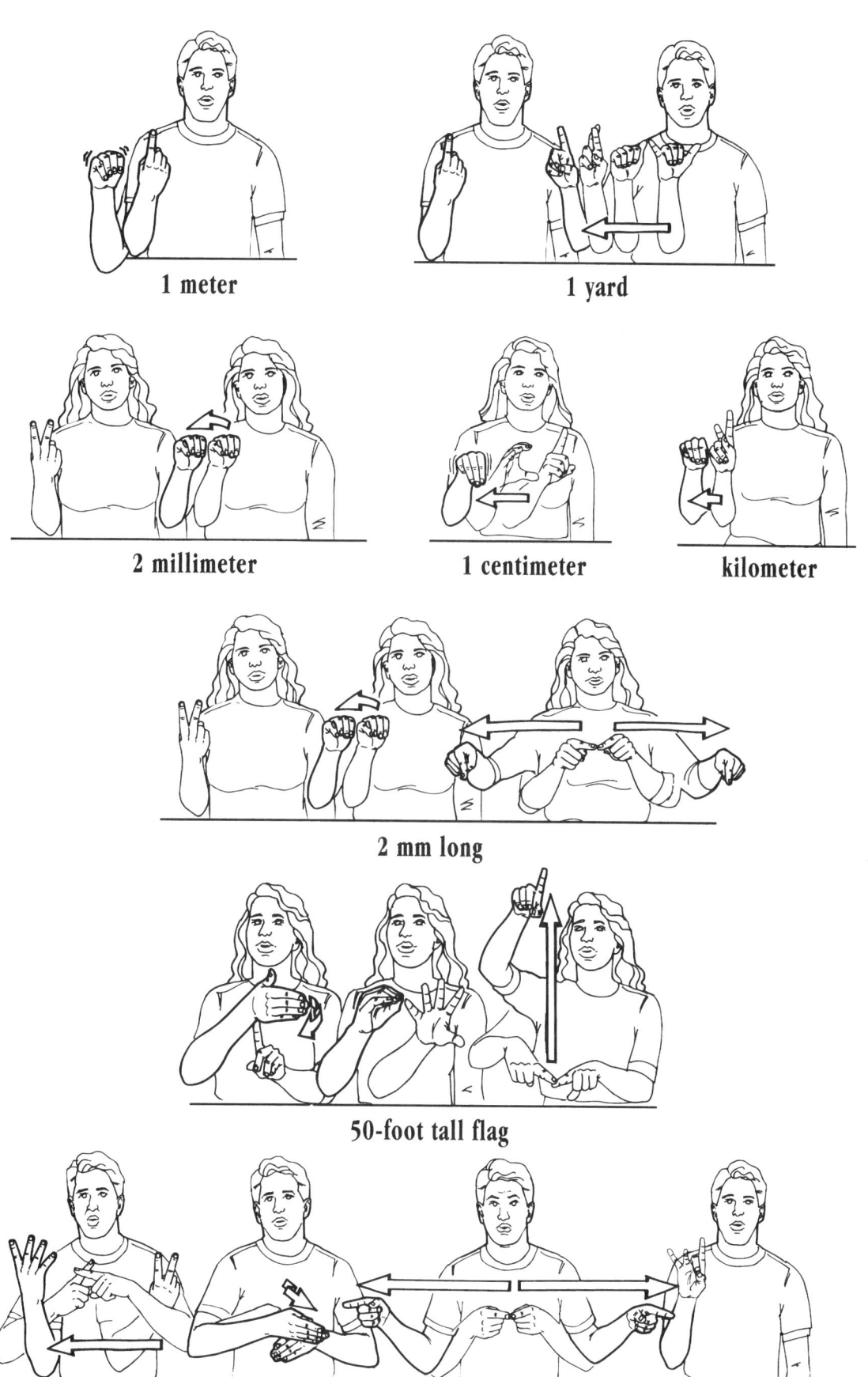

1 meter

1 yard

2 millimeter

1 centimeter

kilometer

2 mm long

50-foot tall flag

8-foot 2 x 4 board

37

Chapter 4

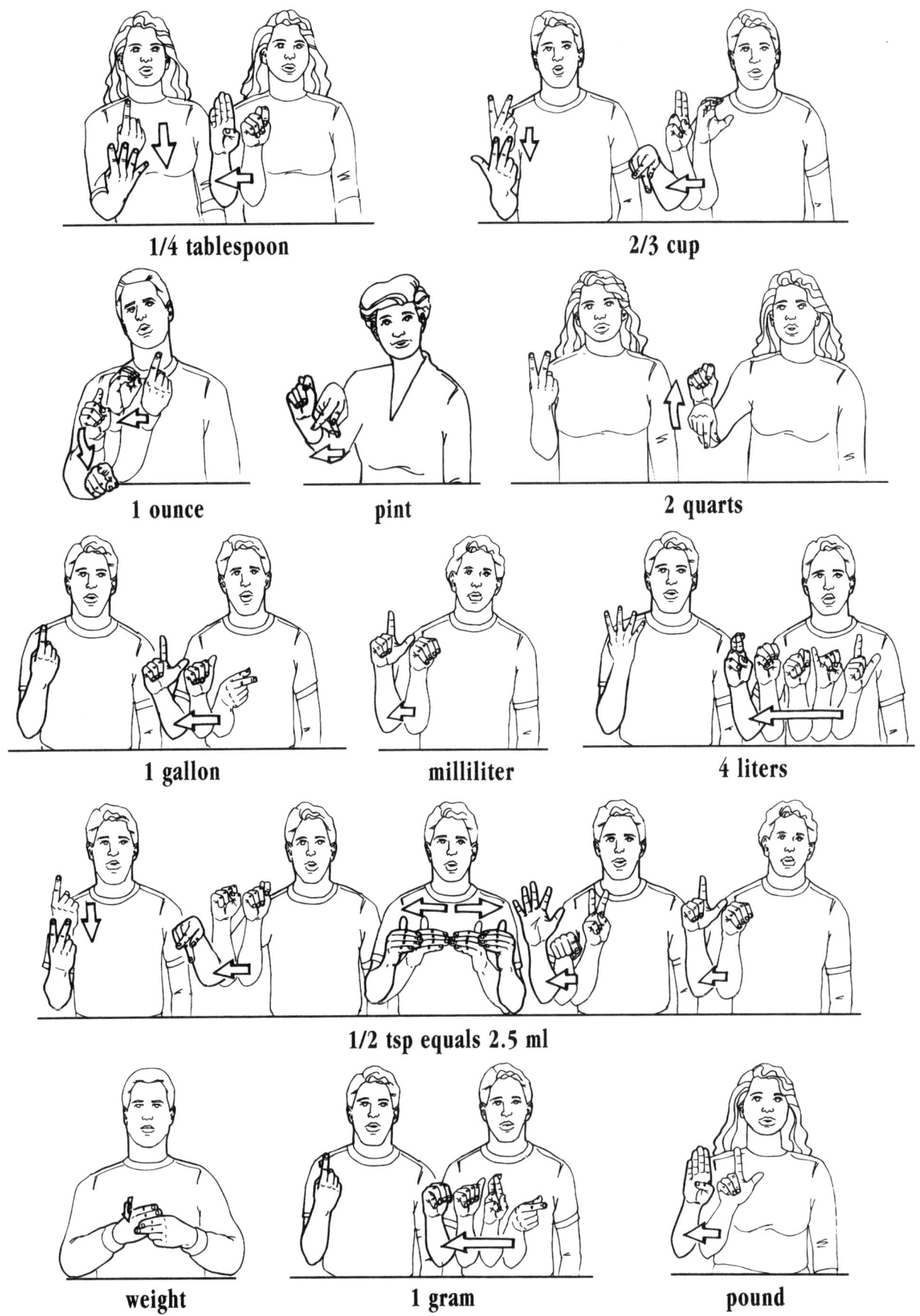

MEASUREMENTS

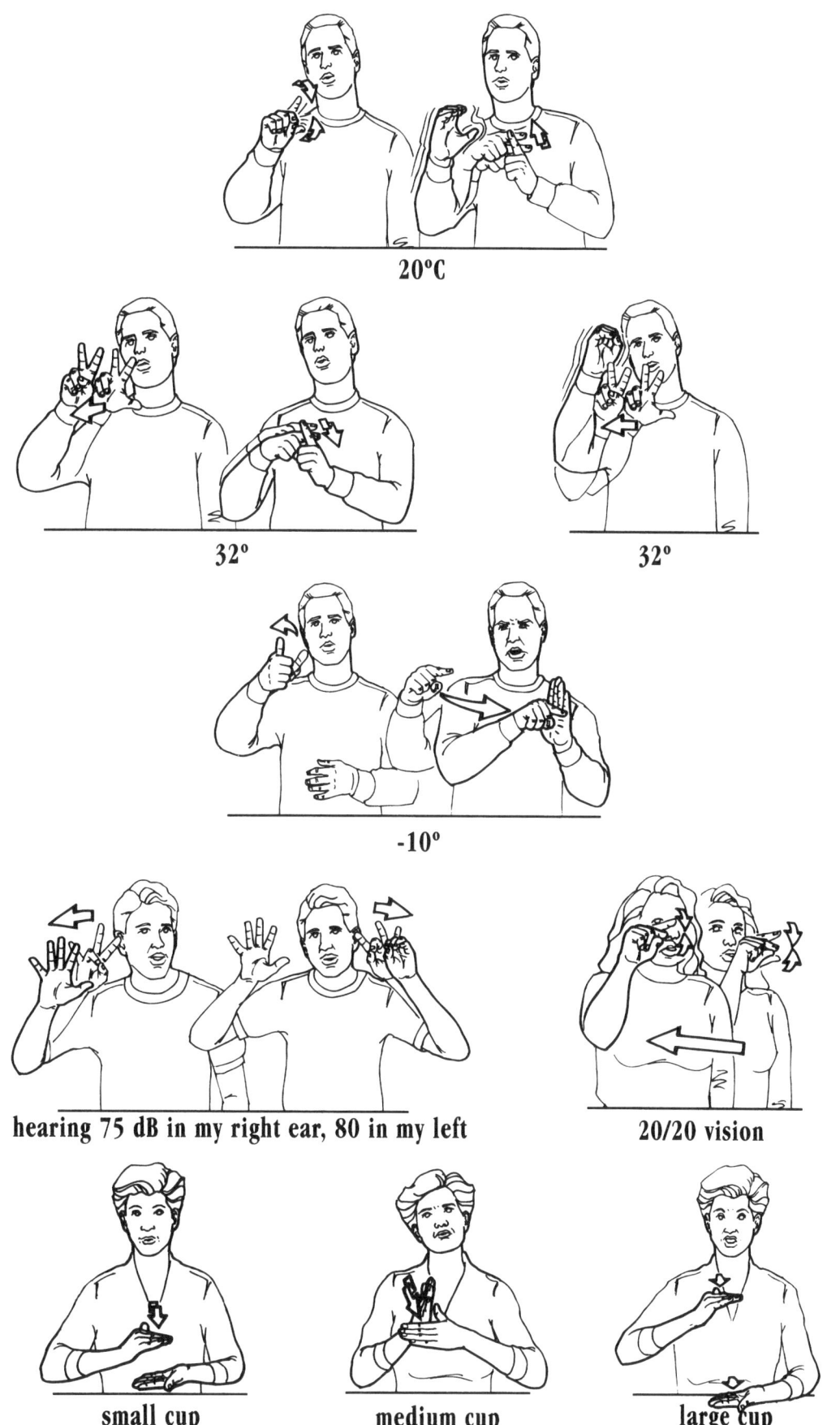

CHAPTER 4

4.5 VEHICLE-RELATED AND COMPUTER-RELATED SIGNS

Fingerspelled abbreviations such as *m-p-h* and *r-p-m* are commonly used in conjunction with numbers to convey vehicle-related information.

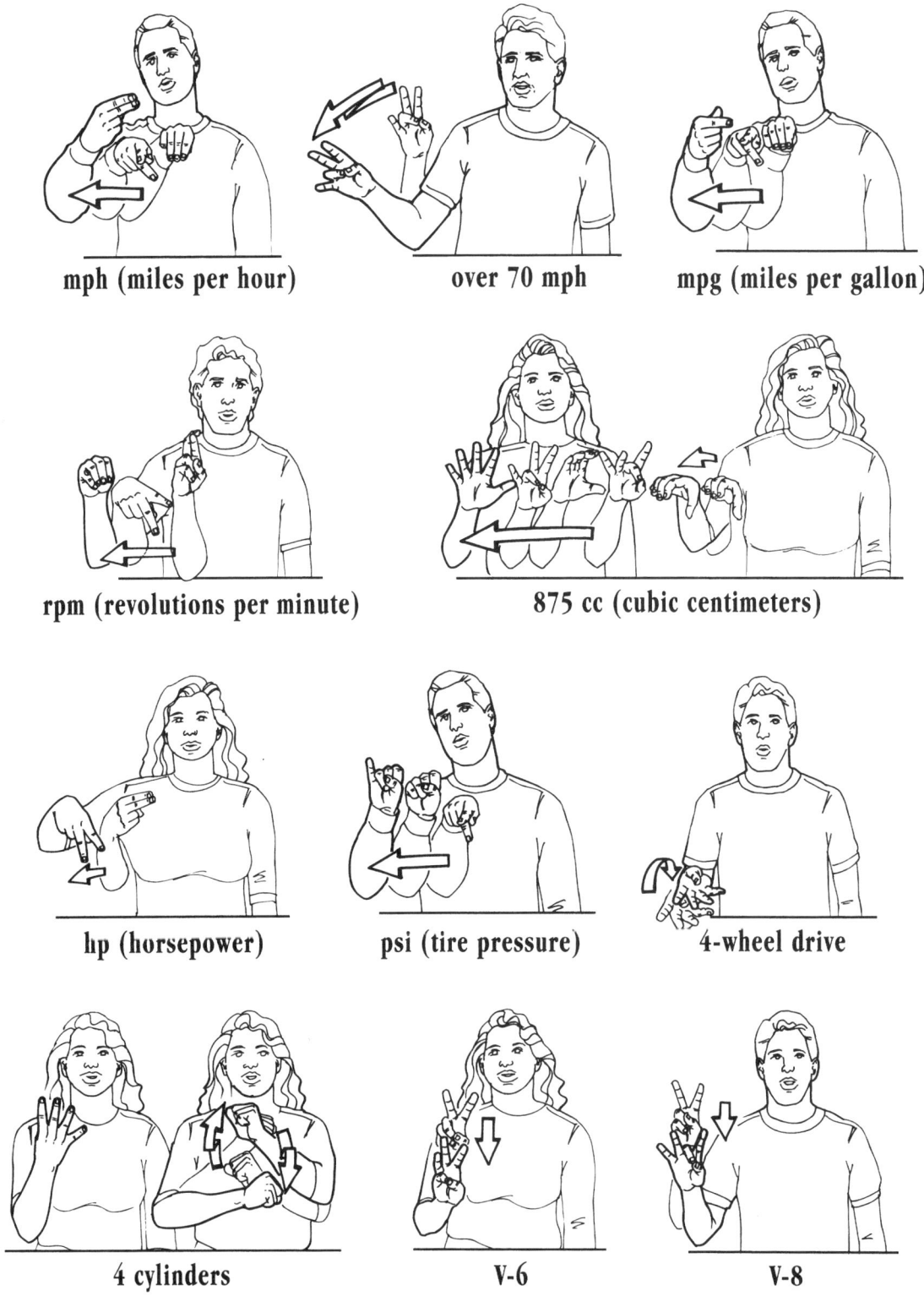

MEASUREMENTS

Phrases Using Vehicle Signs

It is a 65 horsepower engine.

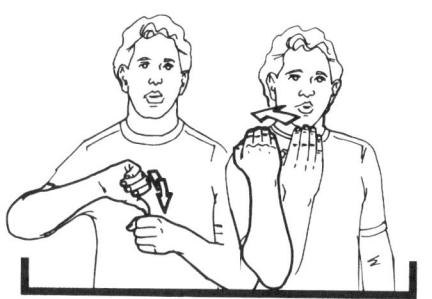

It's a gas guzzler.

My car's mileage is now over 100,000.

The next signs show numbers with abbreviations for high-tech computer concepts, such as *mb* for "megabytes."

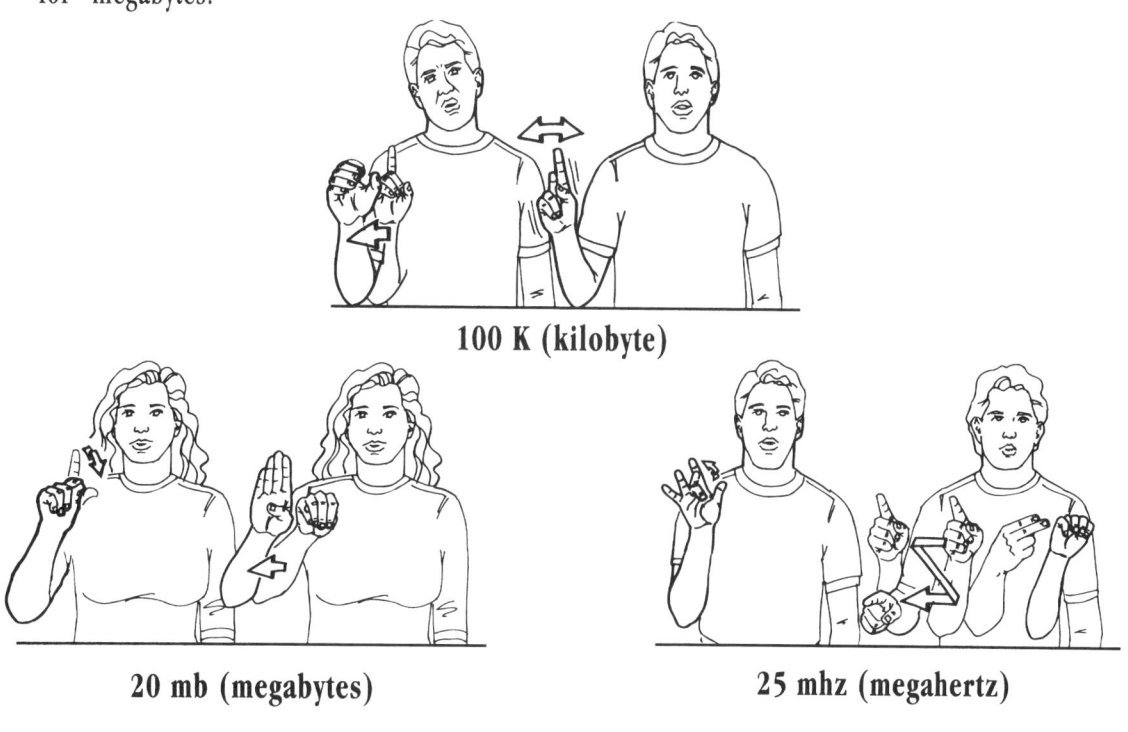

100 K (kilobyte)

20 mb (megabytes)   25 mhz (megahertz)

Chapter 5
How Long

THIS chapter discusses the ways to sign time units. For most units of time in ASL there is a Rule of Nine, where any number from 1 to 9 is incorporated into the sign for the time unit. For example, *two minutes* incorporates the handshape for *two* into the sign for *minute*. For numbers 10 and greater, the number is signed and then the singular sign for the time unit is signed separately.

Seconds

5.1

Second is most often fingerspelled as *S-E-C*.

3 s-e-c

Minutes, Hours, Days, Weeks, and Months

5.2

The sign for *minutes* follows the Rule of Nine, but signers may optionally fingerspell it as *M-I-N*. Following are several examples of signing *minutes*.

1 minute

3 minutes

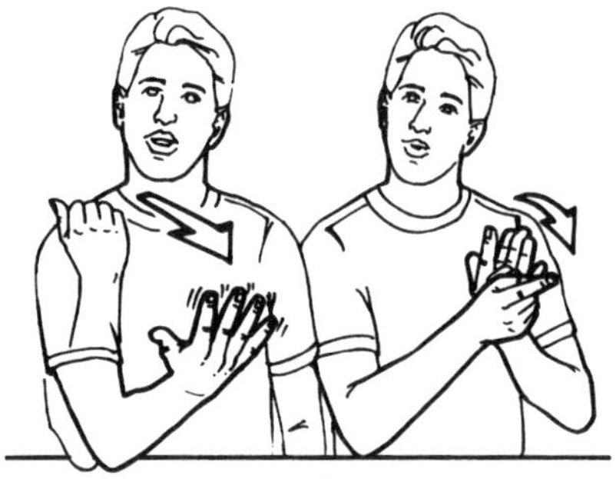

Chapter 5

15 minutes

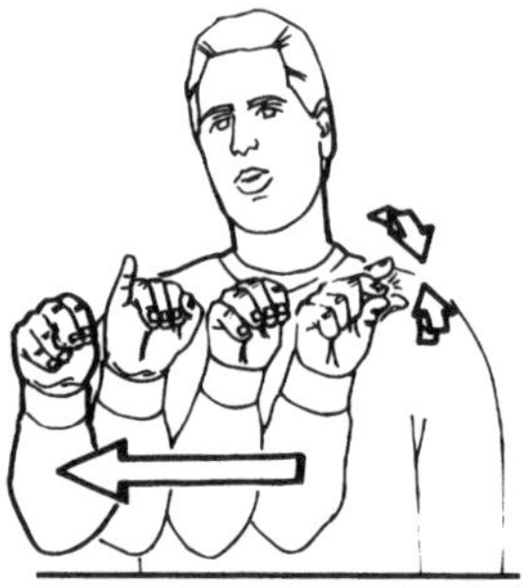

20 minutes

The sign for *hour* follows the Rule of Nine. Following are examples of ways to sign *hour*.

1/2 hour

1 hour

2 hours

4 hours

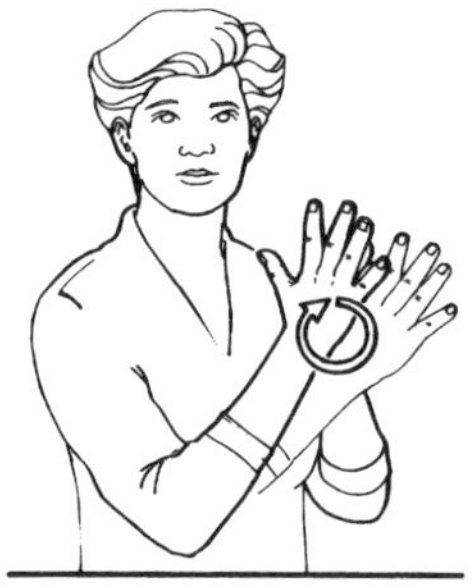

5 hours

24 hours

Here are examples of *day*.

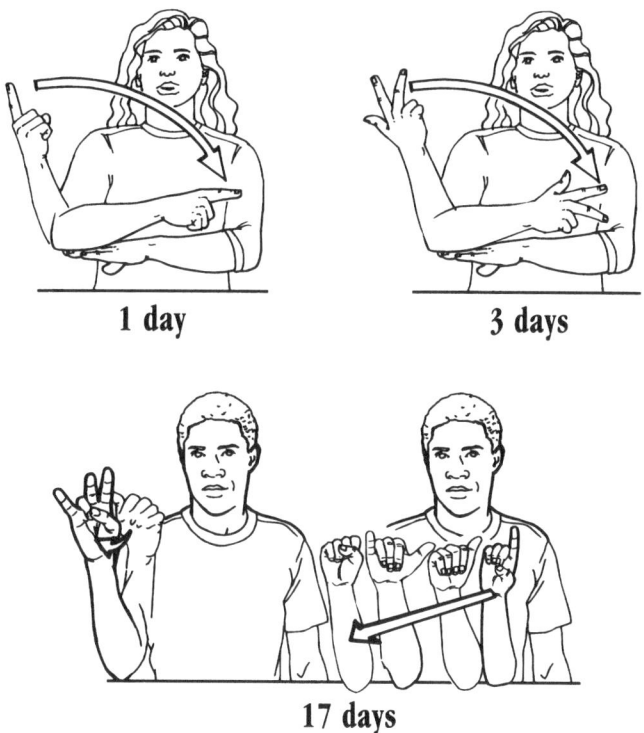

1 day   **3 days**

17 days

Week follows the Rule of Nine. Here are sign examples using *week*.

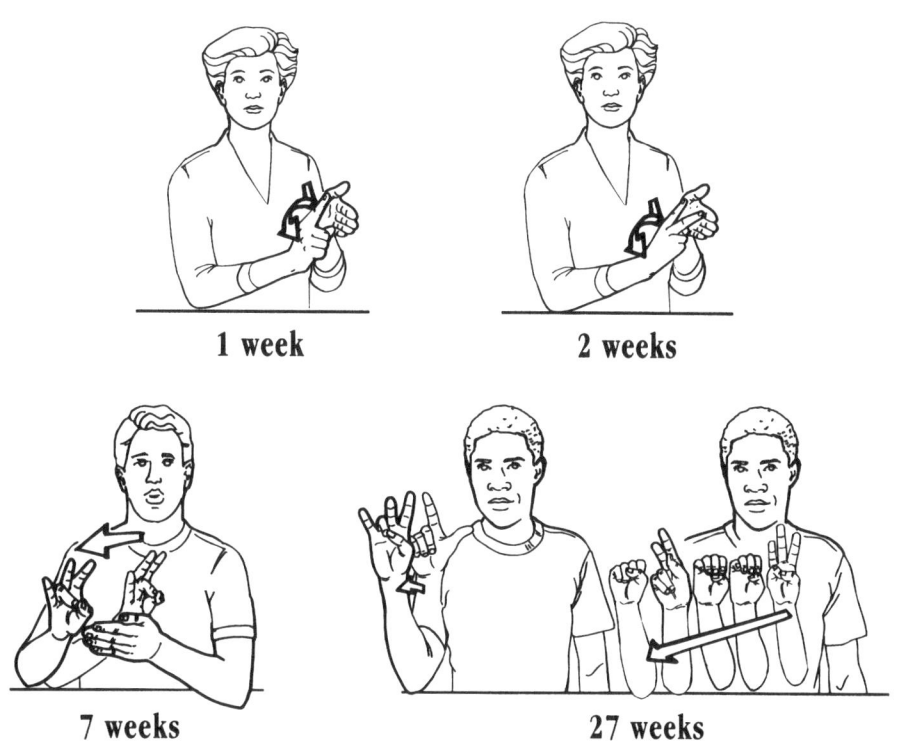

1 week   **2 weeks**

7 weeks   **27 weeks**

The sign for *month* also follows the Rule of Nine. Here are examples of *month*.

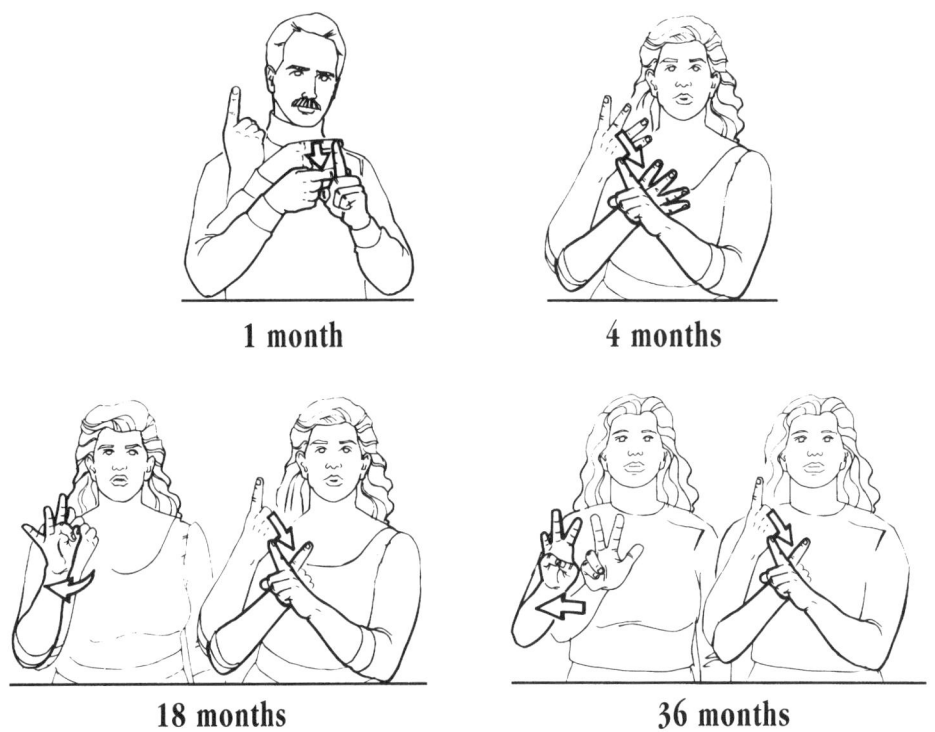

5.3 YEARS

Year does not use the Rule of Nine. Here are examples of *year*.

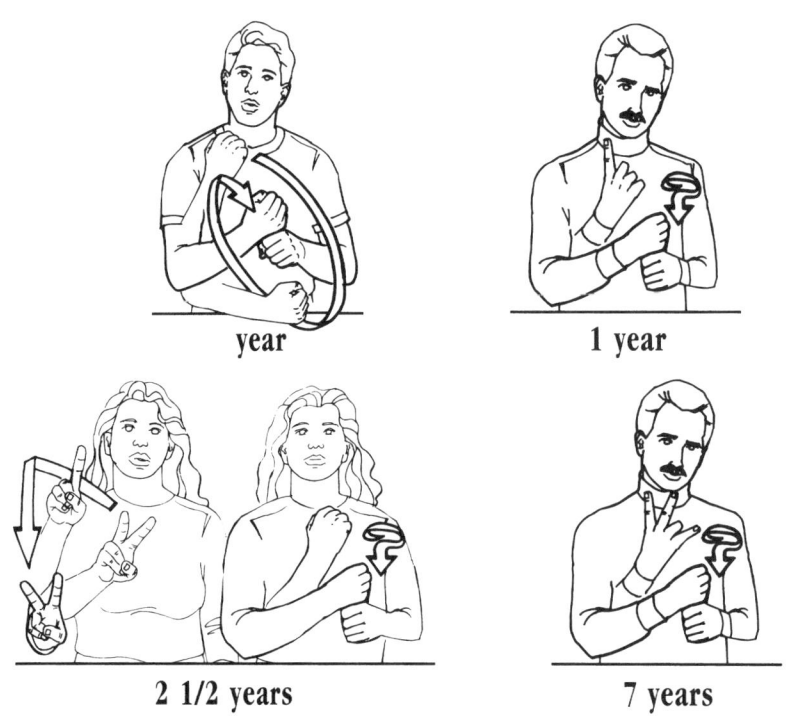

DURATION

Signing time units in terms of duration shows how long something lasts. In English, it is possible to convey a feeling of normal length, "it lasted an hour," or express that an event felt as if it took a long time, "it lasted an *hour*." Emphatic forms of signs using motion and expression convey this same meaning. Following are examples of signs for time that show duration.

1 whole hour

7 long hours

3 whole days

3 long weeks

7 weeks!

1 whole month

4 long months

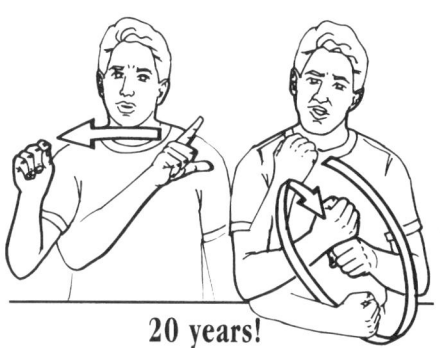
20 years!

Phrases Using Time Duration Signs

How long?

I drove and drove for 3 days.

I waited and waited for 15 minutes!

I was sick for 3 weeks!

How long have you worked for that company?

Four months!

HOW LONG

How long have you two been married?

We've been married for 20 years!

Other Time Vocabulary

all day   all morning   all afternoon

all evening   all night   year-round/all year

Chapter 5

CHAPTER 6
HOW OFTEN

WHEN something happens at regular intervals, it can be described as occurring, for example, "every hour" or "every two hours." ASL expresses these meanings with special signs, based on a number handshape, a time unit, and repeated movement.

NUMERICAL TIME FREQUENCY SIGNS

6.1

One week is a period of time, and the repetition of the sign *1 week* shows that something happens "weekly" or "every week." The signs that follow show how to combine the elements of a number handshape, time unit, and movement when talking about frequency.

every 2 minutes   every 1/2 hour   every 4 hours

everyday   every Monday   every 5 days

Chapter 6

HOW OFTEN

Phrases Using Time Frequency Signs

How often?

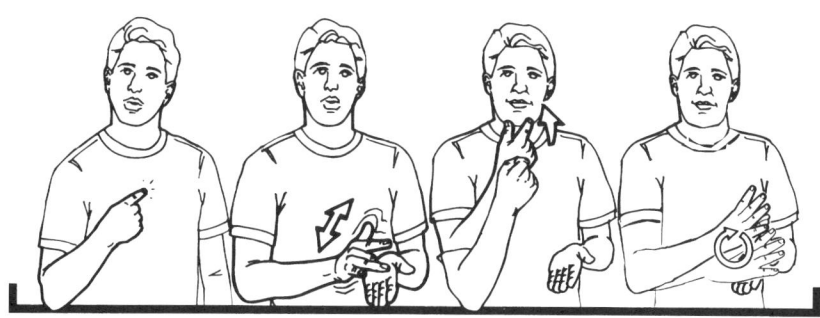

I take medication every 4 hours.

I tend to go out to eat every other week.

I call my mother once a month.

CHAPTER 6

The meeting occurs twice a year.

Presidential elections are held every 4 years.

6.2 OTHER FREQUENCY SIGNS

Some signs that discuss frequency do not use a combination of number handshape, time sign, and repeated movements. These signs describe frequency in more general terms like "always."

HOW OFFEN

first time | many times

regularly | every other weekend

Other Phrases Using Time Frequency Signs

I work 9 to 5 daily.

I've seen that many times.

CHAPTER 7
WHEN

IF you ask someone when an event occurred, the answer could contain a time, a date, or both. The information in this chapter deals with times and dates and explains ASL's physical timeline.

SIGNS FOR TELLING TIME

7.1

Signs for telling time ("1 o'clock," "2 o'clock") are made up of a version of the sign *time* plus a number sign from 1 to 12.

When signing *1 o'clock* through *5 o'clock*, remember that this is an instance in which the first five numbers appear palm-outward.

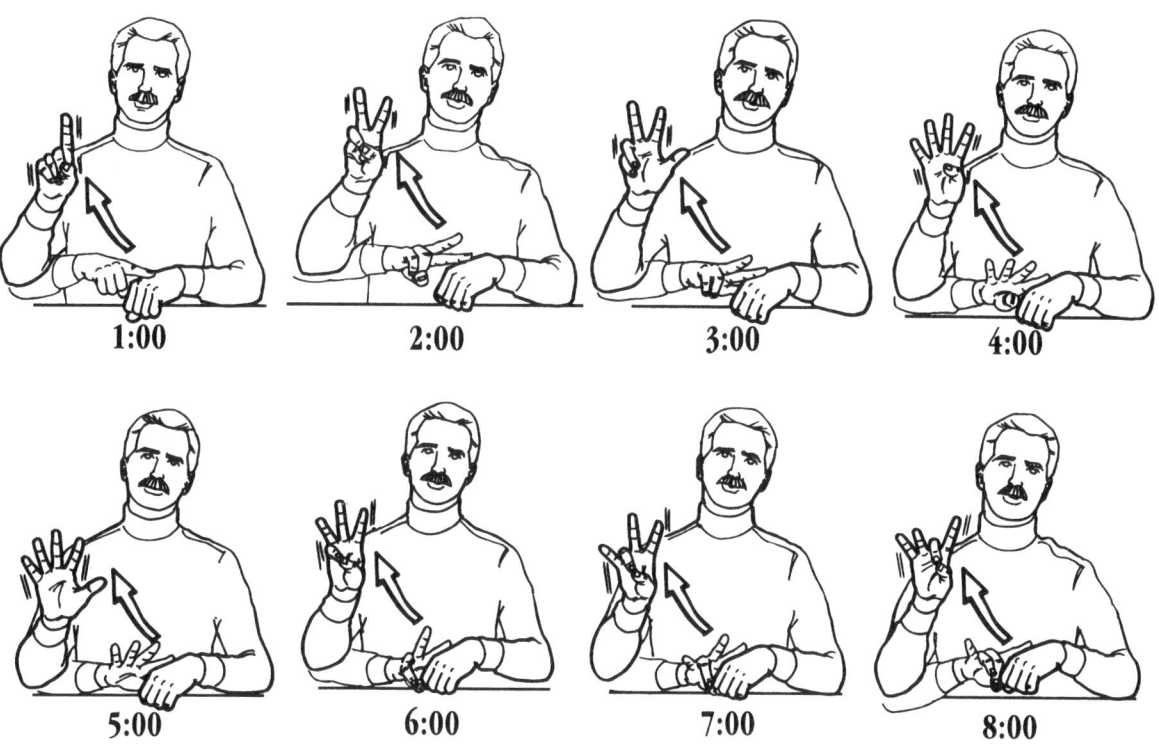

CHAPTER 7

9:00    10:00    11:00 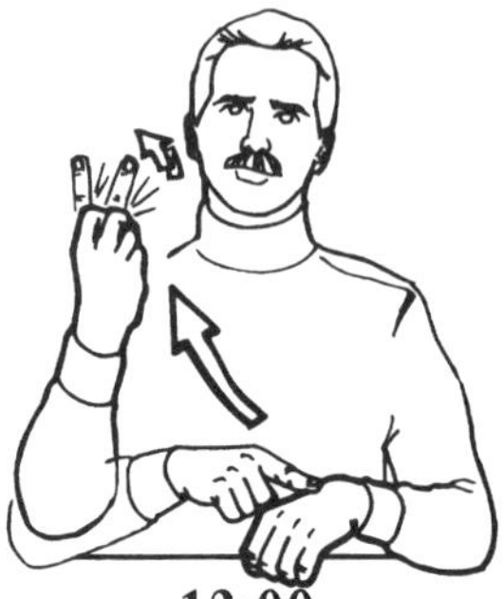   12:00

11:30    12:05

1:15

7.2 TIME ESTIMATES

When it is necessary to express an approximate time, facial expression or a sign that suggests something will happen "around" 2 o'clock is used.

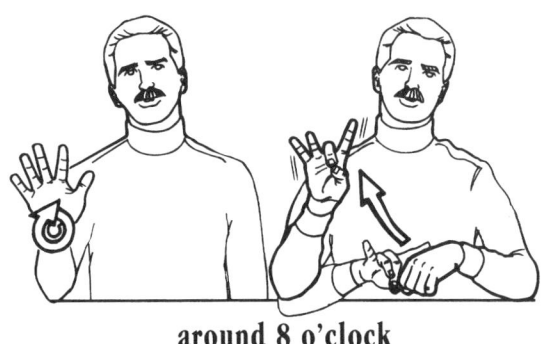

around 8 o'clock

WHEN

Phrases Using Time Signs

What is the best time to go?

At 2:00.

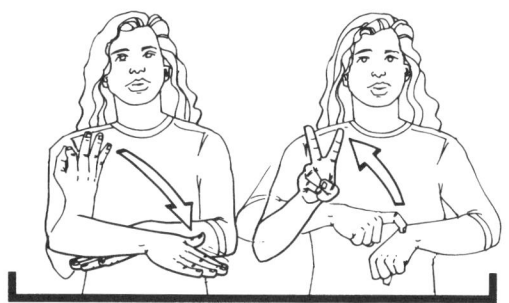

On Friday afternoon at 2:00.

Between 10:00 and 11:00.

Chapter 7

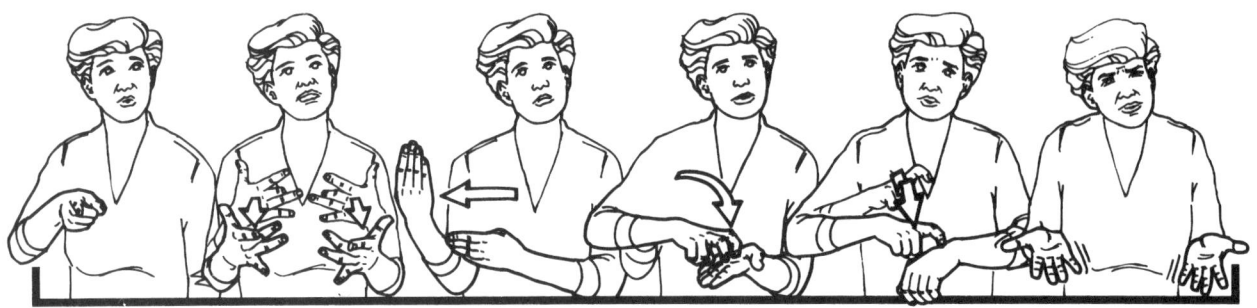

What time in the morning do you usually get up?

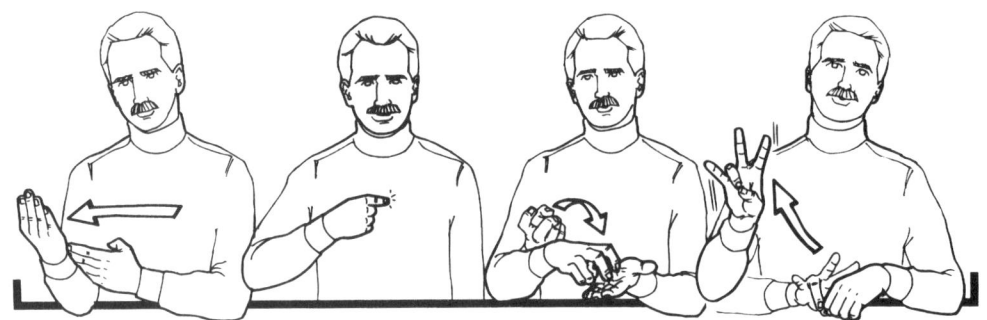

I get up at 7 am every morning.

What time do you work?

I work from 10 am to 3 pm.

The Timeline in ASL

One of the most important uses of space in ASL can be found in the relation of physical space to time. The physical timeline created in ASL has standard locations for the past, the present, and the future. The past is the area behind the signer. Signs such as *yesterday* and *last week* reflect that the area behind the signer represents the past. The future is the area moving out away from the signer. Forward movement in signs such as *will*, *future*, *tomorrow*, and *next week* reflect that the area in front of the signer represents the future. The space directly in front and close to the signer represents the present, as seen in the sign *now*.

Past

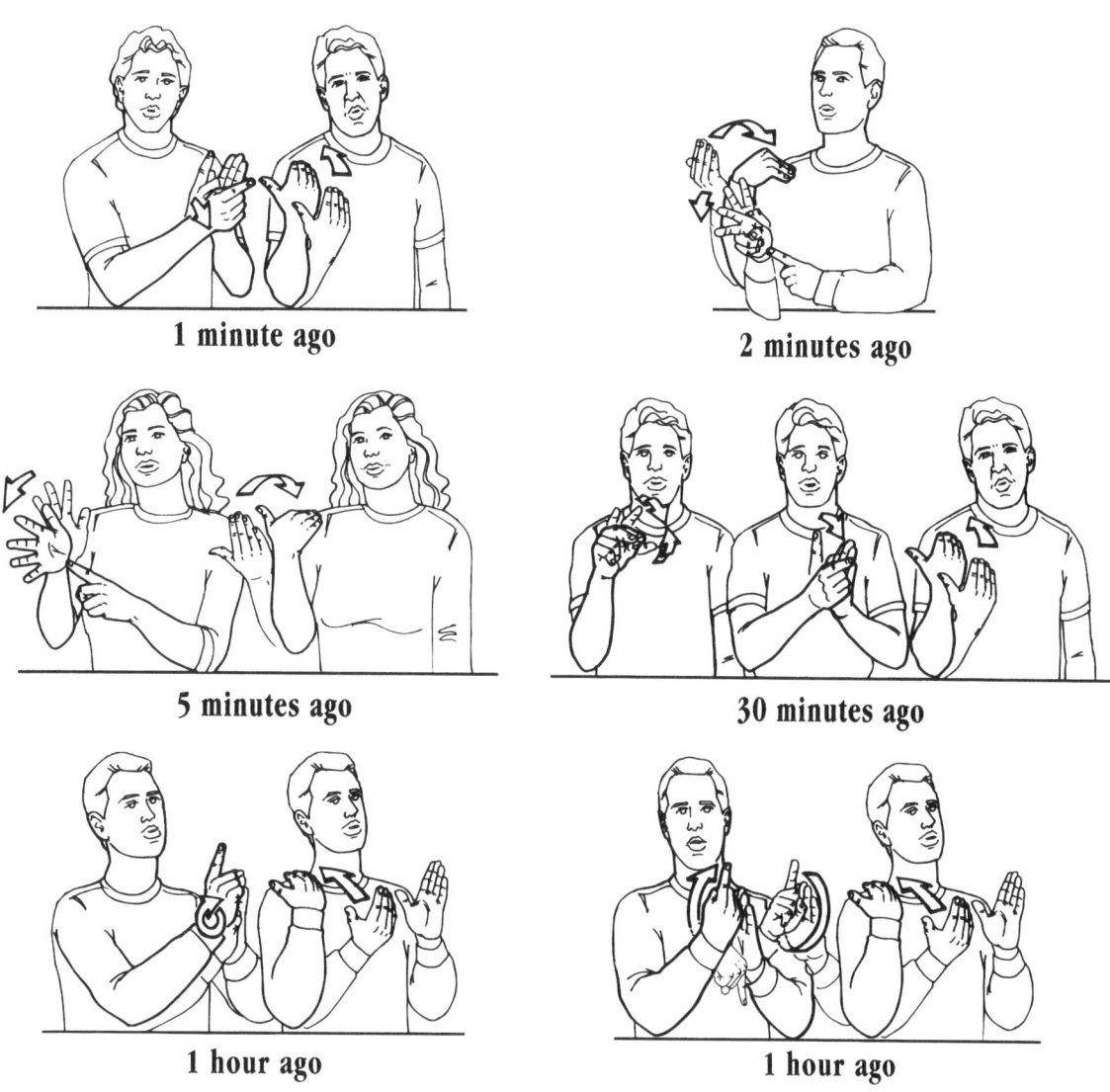

1 minute ago

2 minutes ago

5 minutes ago

30 minutes ago

1 hour ago

1 hour ago

CHAPTER 7

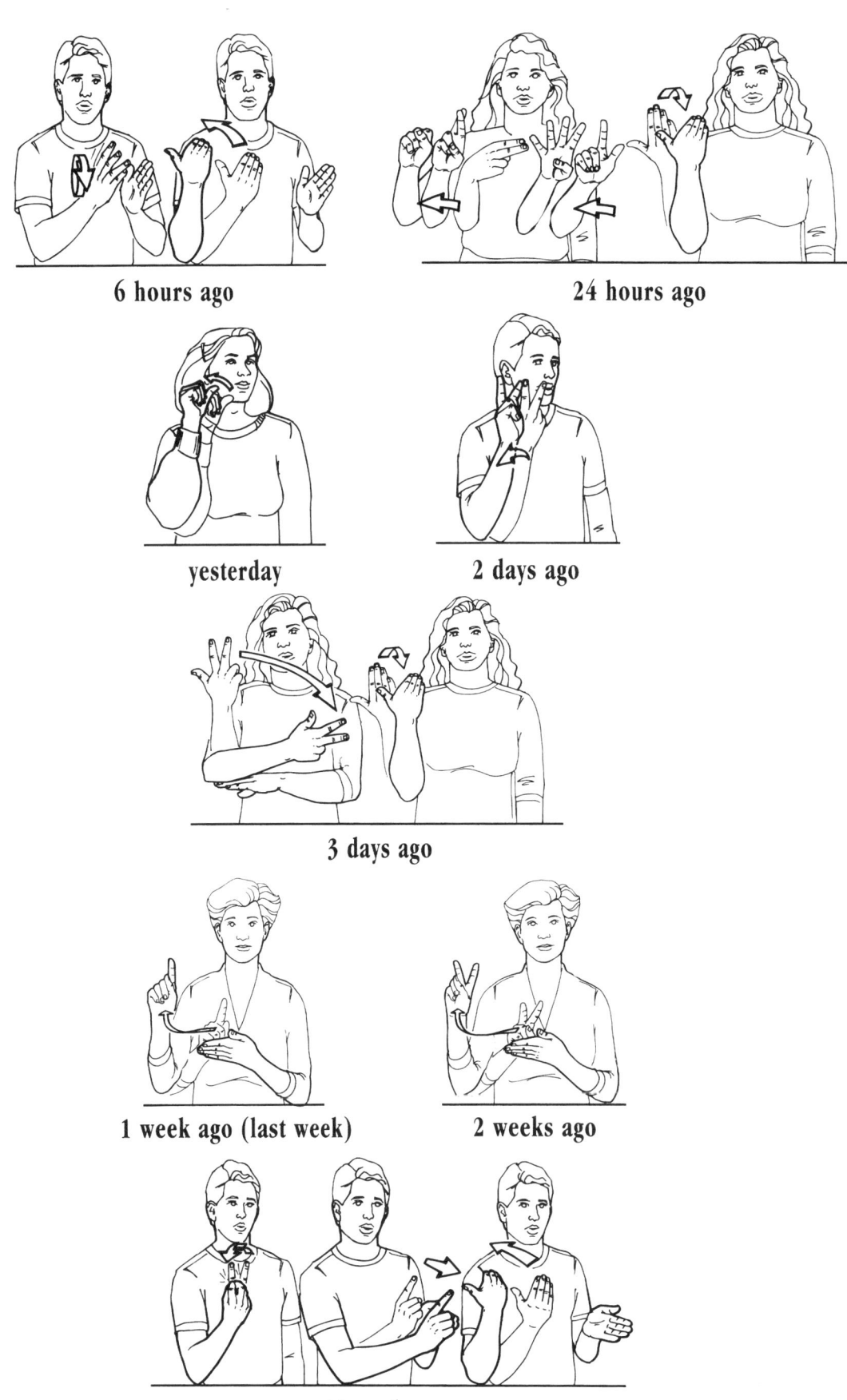

6 hours ago

24 hours ago

yesterday

2 days ago

3 days ago

1 week ago (last week)

2 weeks ago

12 weeks ago

WHEN

Chapter 7

Future

WHEN

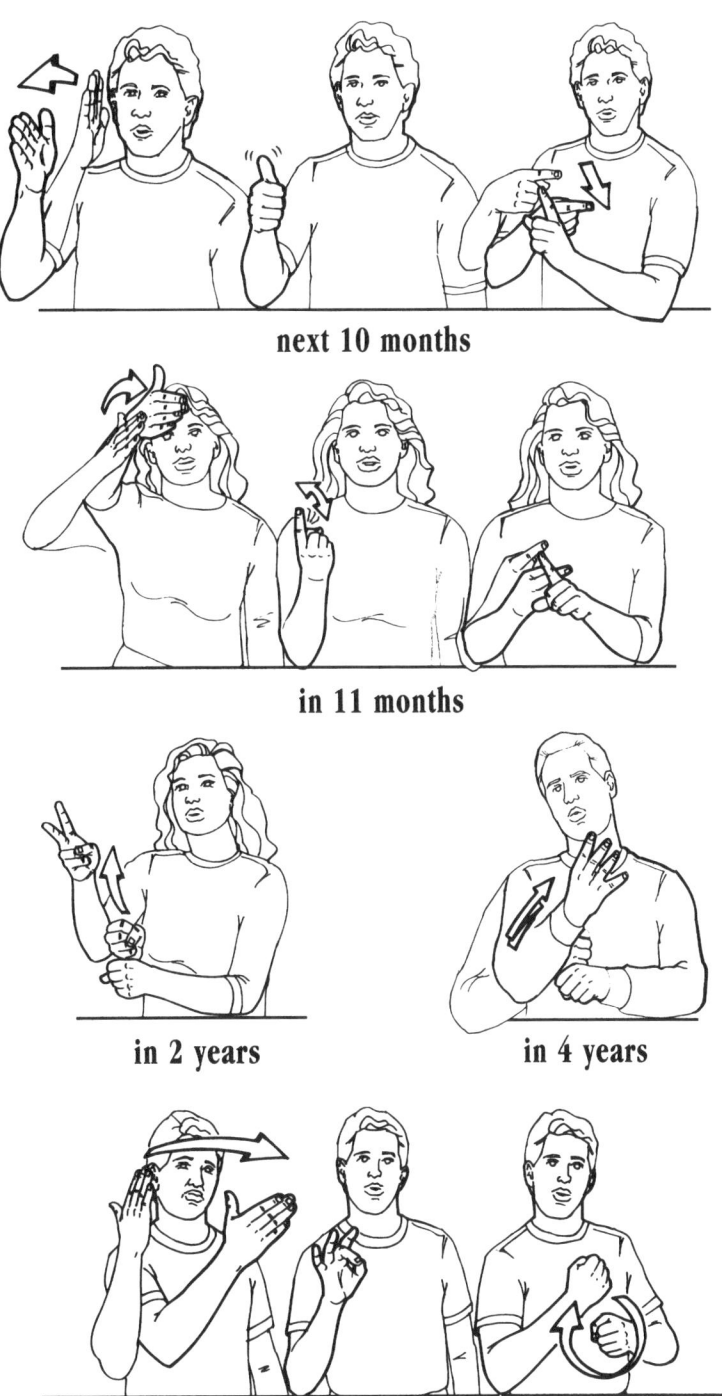

next 10 months

in 11 months

in 2 years

in 4 years

8 years from now

Phrases Using Signs and the Physical Space Timeline

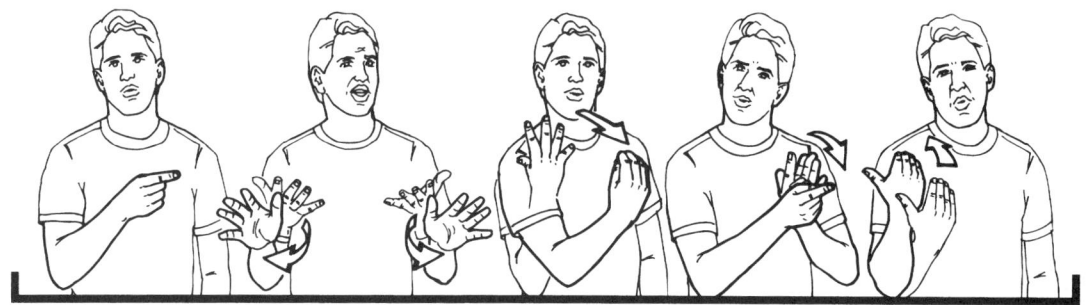

She already left a minute ago.

I just arrived 5 minutes ago.

It will start in 15 minutes.

We'll get it in 2 weeks.

YEAR AND DATE SIGNS

7.4

Years are most often signed as two digit numbers. Nineteen seventy-six is signed 19 for the first two digits, 76 for the second two digits. In years where the second two digits are within the range of 01—09 the zero is emphasized for clarity. Signs for even century years vary depending on context. If speaking generally, the sign for the double zero is the sign for *hundred*. If speaking specifically, the double zero is emphasized.

2000    2000 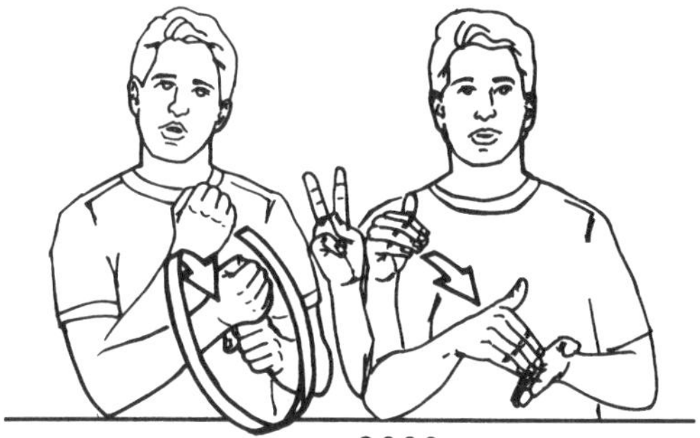   year 2000

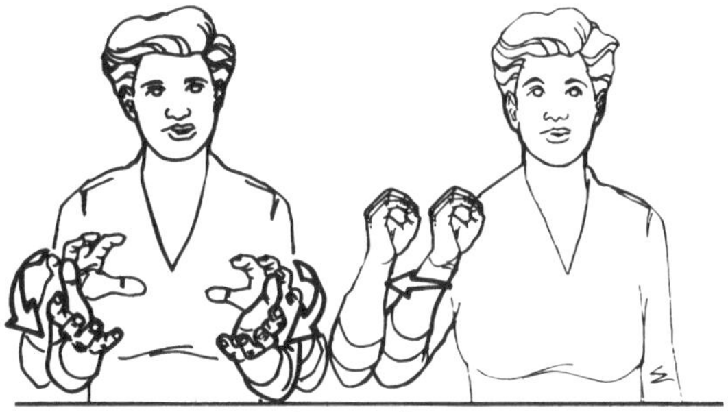

class of '00 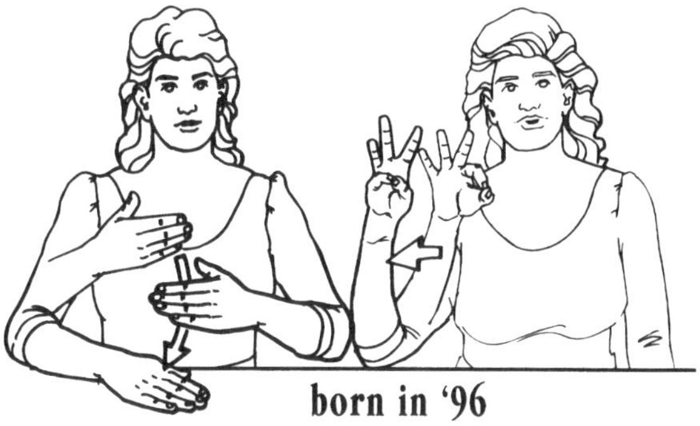   born in '96

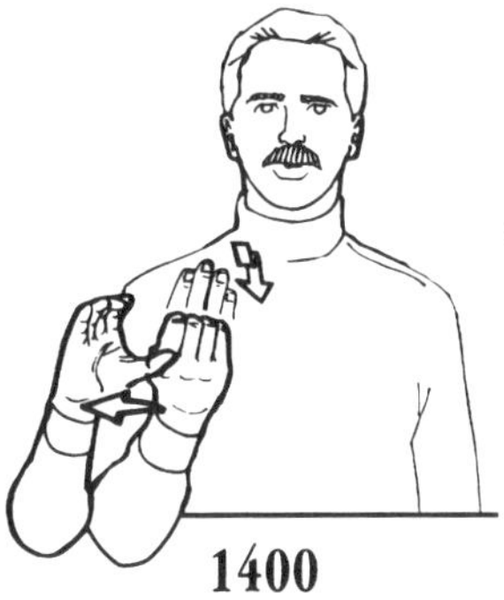

1400    1776    1805    2002

Approximate Signs for Years

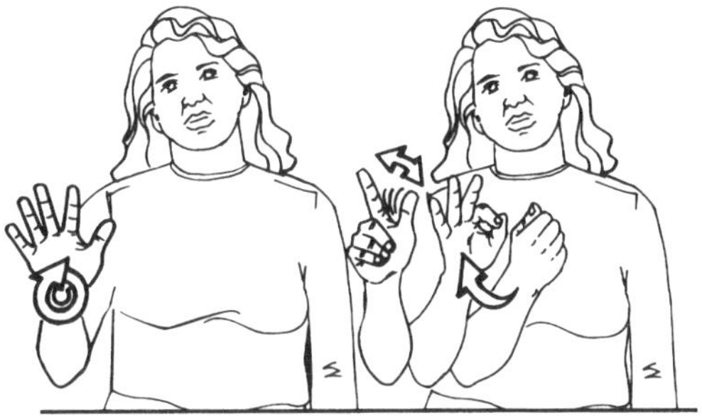

thereabout 1921    1950s

Specific dates with month, day, and year in ASL are easy to sign. First, fingerspell the month (some months are commonly signed as abbreviations):

| J-A-N | F-E-B | M-A-R-C-H | A-P-R-I-L | M-A-Y | J-U-N-E |
| J-U-L-Y | A-U-G | S-E-P-T | O-C-T | N-O-V | D-E-C |

The day of the month is expressed as an ordinal number if it is the first through the ninth day of the month, for instance *J-A-N second* or *N-O-V ninth*. For dates of the tenth through the thirty-first day of the month, a cardinal or counting number is used; for example, *J-u-l-y fourteen* is proper in ASL, and the English equivalent is "July fourteenth."

December 3, 1955

November 8, 2000

1865-1877

1910 to 1983

CHAPTER 8
AGE

◆ ◆ ◆

WHEN someone is asked how old they are, they will answer by telling their age. In ASL age is expressed by combining the movement and location of the sign "old" with the number of years. When talking about age, the numbers 1 through 5 face palm-outward, unlike when counting. Pay careful attention to how the various handshapes touch the chin in the following age signs.

AGE

8.1

1 year old

2 years old

3 years old

4 years old

5 years old

6 years old

7 years old

8 years old

9 years old

CHAPTER 8

Ages Signed with Emphasis

40 years old!

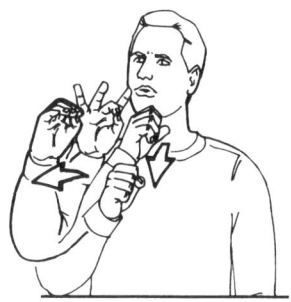
80 years old!

Approximate Signs for Ages

around 30 years old

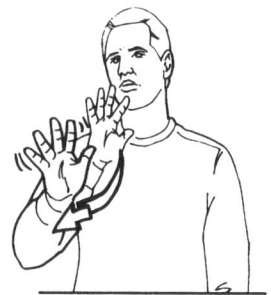
in his/her 50s

Phrases Using Age Signs

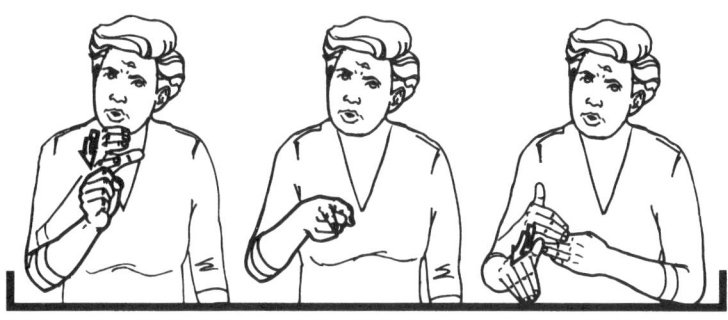
How old is that bread?

5 days old.

Chapter 8

The baby is 8 months old.

My oldest child is now 15 years old.

How old were you when you first flew?

I was 40 years old.

AGE

How old were you when you started reading?

I was 3 years old.

CHAPTER 9
SPORTS

WHEN discussing sports, numbers are used to give information about scores, placement, and players' jersey numbers. Following are both number signs and signs for additional vocabulary related to sports.

SPORTS-RELATED VOCABULARY

9.1

Baseball

Chapter 9

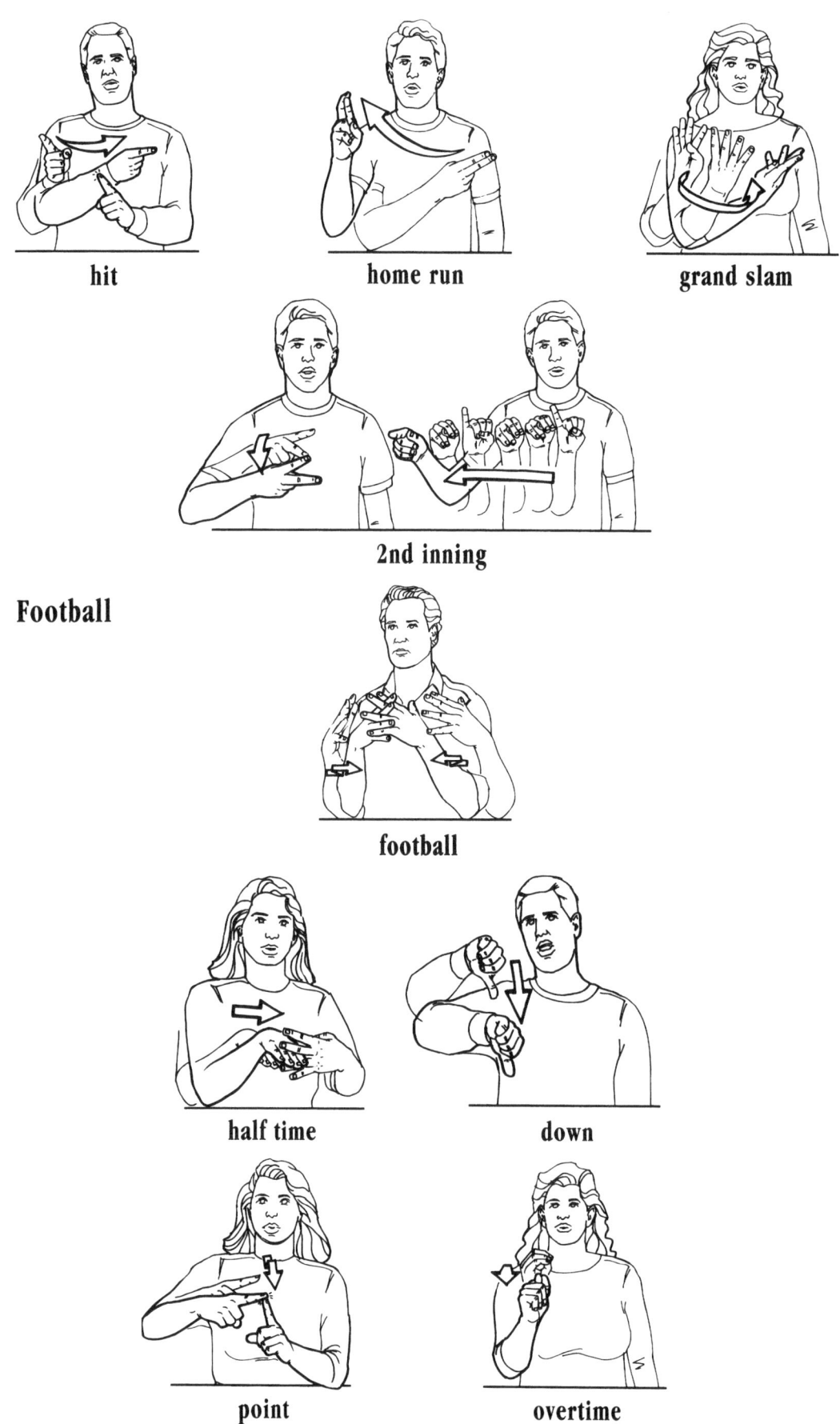

Football

Track

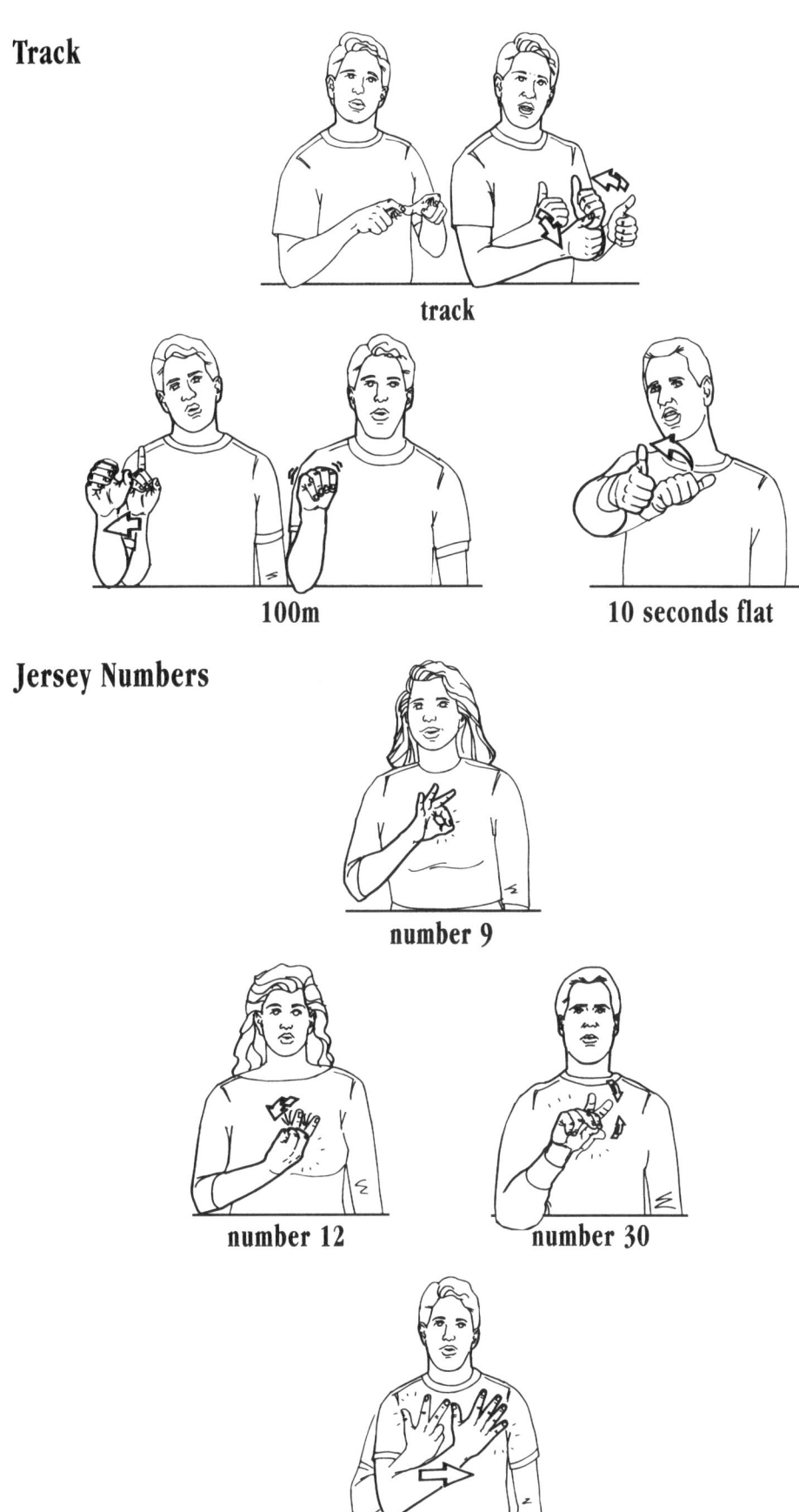

track

100m

10 seconds flat

Jersey Numbers

number 9

number 12

number 30

number 35

CHAPTER 9

9.2 PLACEMENT AND SCORES

In ASL, ordinal numbers with a horizontal movement to indicate place are used to express who wins a competition or a how a person or team has finished.

SPORTS

Phrases About Placement and Scores

What is the score?

The second team won 5 to 2.

Did you win?

I finished third.

Signs about teams and their scores use space to represent one team against another.

my team 3, their team 5

score 3 to 0

Chapter 9

CHAPTER 10
WHERE, WHICH

THIS chapter includes vocabulary for describing specifics, such as where to find a particular book, which hat you prefer, and the address of your favorite restaurant.

LOCATION

10.1

Numbers used to locate an object, such as a book on a particular shelf of a bookcase, or a specific car in a parking lot combine ASL's use of physical space with ordinal number signs. Spatial patterns are used to describe locations. Two patterns that occur frequently are (1) a straight-downward pattern, in which each item is on a different line, like shelves in a bookcase that are stacked one below the other, and (2) a straight-sideways pattern, similar to a row of books on a shelf or to cars in one aisle of a parking lot. The following signed locations give the physical location that tells you where and the ordinal number that describes which.

first shelf

fourth drawer down below

eighth hat up there

Chapter 10

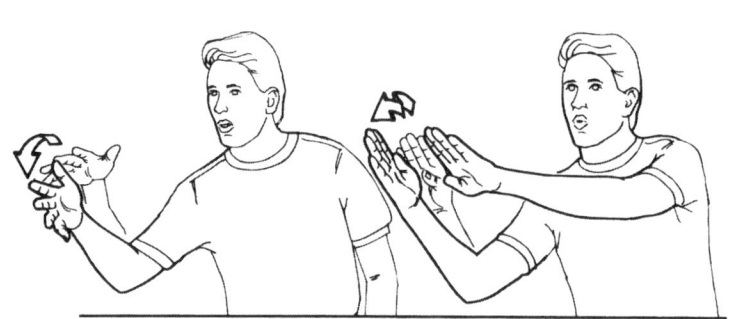
fifth door to the right

third car

downstairs on the second floor

upstairs on the tenth floor

PLACES

10.2

The following signs show how to describe locations by street names. In numbered street names, there is an important difference between English and ASL. English uses ordinal numbers, such as "22nd Street" or "35th Avenue" for numbered streets. ASL more often uses a cardinal (counting) number sign for numbered streets above "Ninth," for example, *Twenty-two Street* or *Thirty-five A-V-E*. Note that these are names nonetheless and the "nd" or "th" part of the street name that English speakers pronounce is understood in ASL without adding the ordinal information.

the intersection of 5th and Washington

22nd Street and 35th Avenue

RANK OR ORDER IN FAMILY

10.3

When discussing family, it is common to talk about siblings and yourself in terms of birth order, who was born first, second, third, and so on. A signer represents the number of people being discussed on one hand, showing by number how many people are involved, and then explains their order from the thumb (first in order) on down. This method of describing order is not limited to the family, however, the following signs are examples of rank or order in the family. Also shown are signs for *twin* and *only child*.

twin

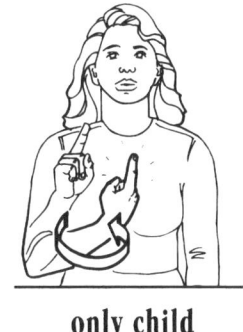

only child

CHAPTER 10

Phrases Showing Order in Family

She is an only child.

I am the second of 3 children.

I am the sixth child of 7 children.

Out of 8 brothers and sisters, I am the last child born.

My son is the third of my 5 children.

WHERE, WHICH

ORDINAL NUMBERS

10.4

As shown in previous chapters, ordinal numbers explain the position of something in an ordered set or group. Following are ASL's basic signs for ordinal numbers that show placement, rank, or order.

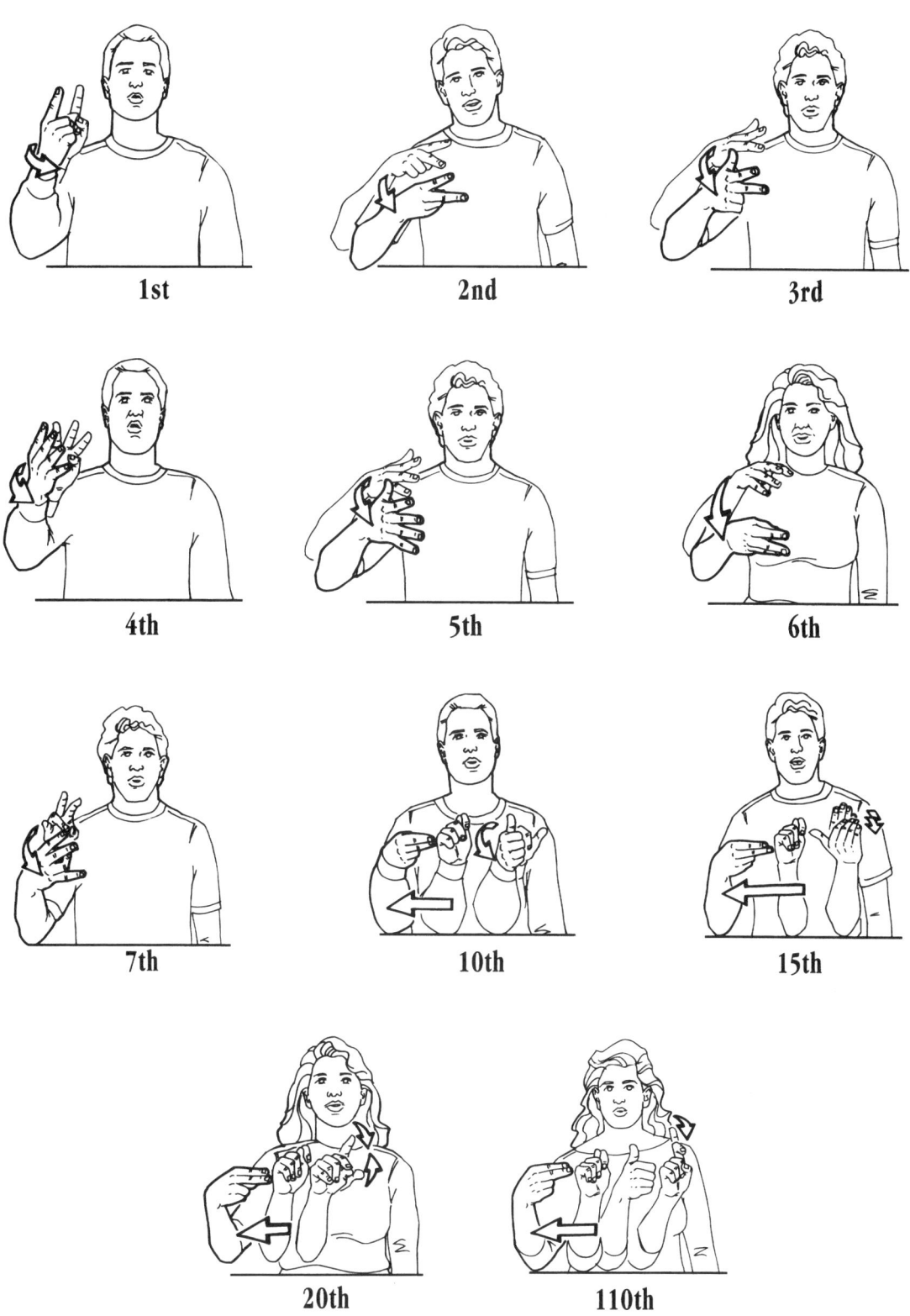

CHAPTER 10

Phrases for Sequence of Events

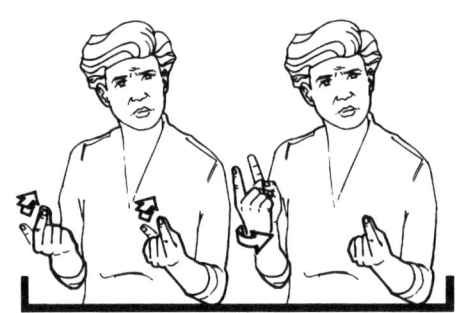

What did you do first?

What did you do first?

first   second   third

CHAPTER 11
PERSONAL NUMBERS

NUMBERS are often used to give information; addresses, phone numbers, and social security numbers are all numbers that people use in their personal lives.

IDENTIFICATION NUMBERS

11.1

Personal identification numbers do not represent quantities and are therefore signed differently than quantitative numbers. For example, a TTY number or a street address is signed more like a fingerspelled word. The street number "1524" would be signed as *1-5-2-4*, rather than as *one thousand five hundred twenty-four*. In this case, the numbers 1 through 5 are signed palm-out, not palm-inward as in counting. In ASL, it is also possible to combine two-digit groups, so "1524" can be signed *fifteen twenty-four*. The two signs appear as regular ASL number signs, as shown in Chapter 1.

Phone Numbers

716-3929

(TTY number) 482-3006

Social Security Numbers

163-10-9119

309-77-0825

Addresses

address34518 Taos Road

2341 Pine Street

PERSONAL NUMBERS

SIGNS FOR SPECIFIC THINGS

11.2

Ordinal numbers with a wiggling movement are used in ASL when discussing one-digit room numbers, TV channels, or highway numbers.

Which channel is it?

It's channel 7.

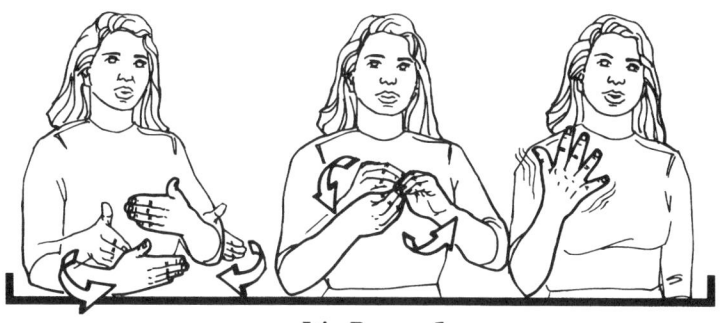
It's Room 5.

Highway 1

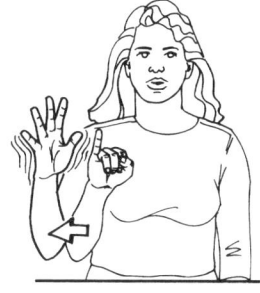
I-5

CHAPTER 12
SCIENTIFIC NUMBERS

THE following are examples of vocabulary used in math and science. Mathematical and chemical formulas, which are often written with superscript and subscript numbers, are usually signed in ASL so their spatial layout is reflected.

SCIENTIFIC NUMBERS

12.1

scientific number

math

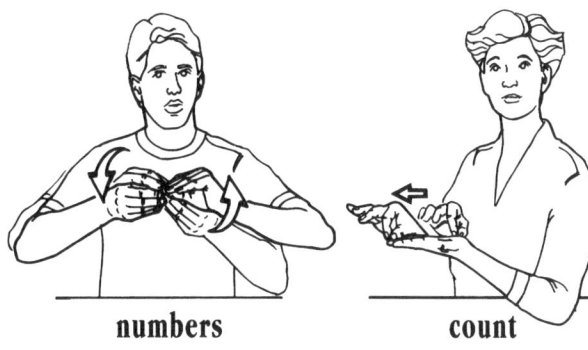
numbers

count

equal

left

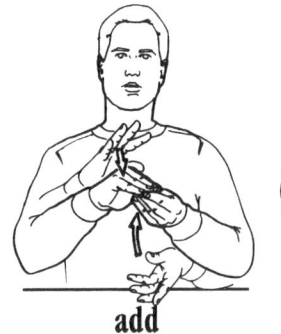
add

subtract

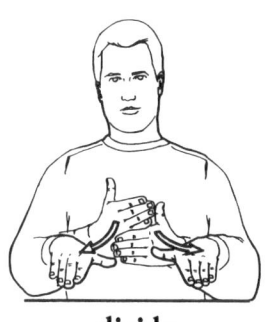
multiply divide

SCIENTIFIC NUMBERS

square root

square root

Phrases Using Scientific Number Signs

Do you like math?

Three and 9 is 12.

Four times 8 equals 32.

Eleven and 9, adds up to 20.

Two times 2 is how many?

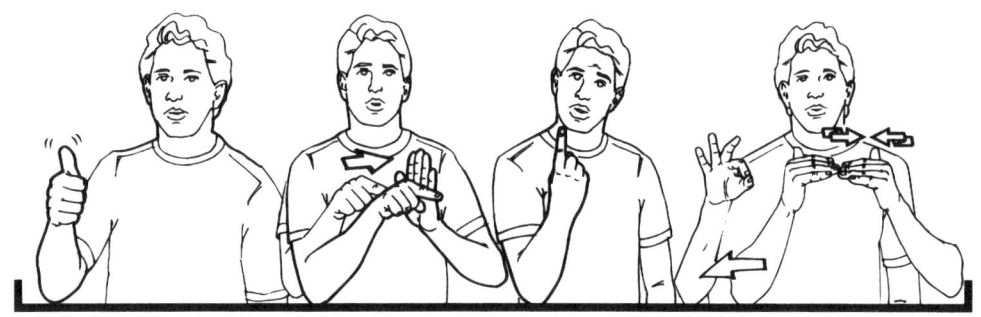
Ten minus 1 equals 9.

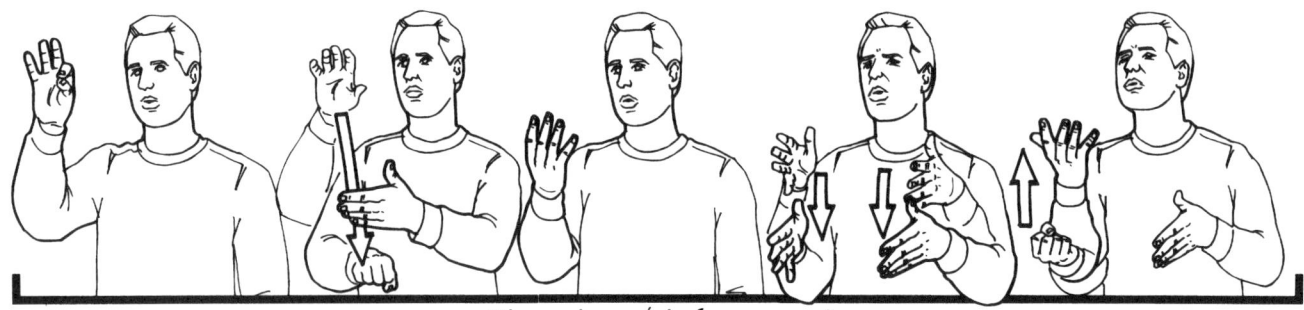
Nine minus 4 is how many?

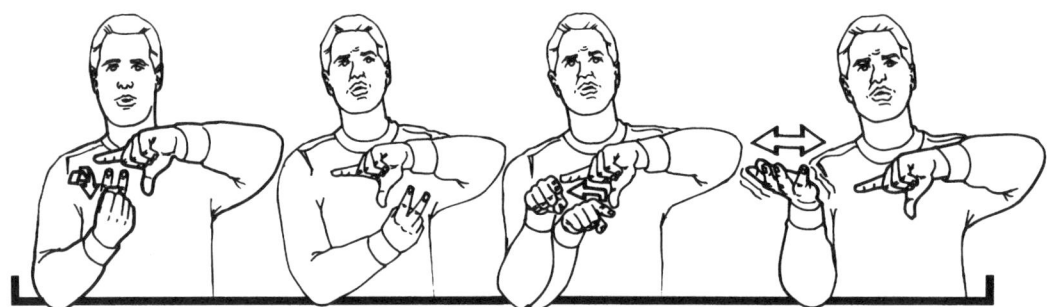
Twelve divided by 2 equals what?

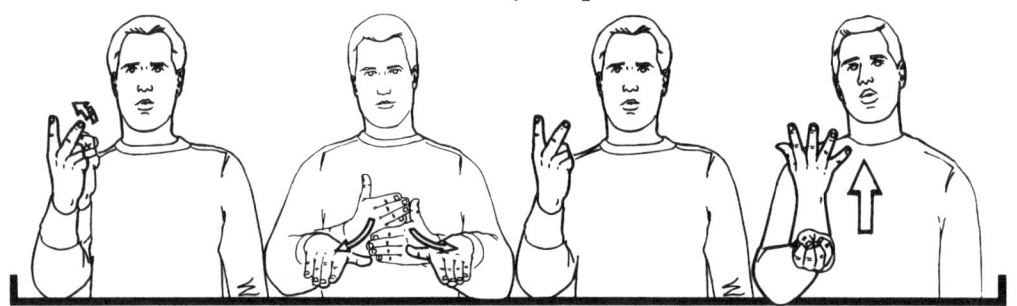
Twelve divided by 2 is how many?

X^2 plus Y^2 equals Z^2

SCIENTIFIC NUMBERS

chemistry

CO_2

CO_2

H_2O

NOTES

NOTES